More Adventures of a Psychic Nurse

Haunted Hospitals!

SHIRLEY SMOLKO, RN, BSN, MBA, MSA

Joe Smolko, M.Ed.

Cavallaro Publishing

MORE ADVENTURES OF A
PSYCHIC NURSE

Disclaimers

This book is narrative nonfiction and should be considered a literary work. It reflects my present recollections of experiences over time. Events have been compressed, and all dialogue has been recreated to represent what may have been said. Therefore, the dialogue in this memoir should be considered representative dialogue. I have tried to recreate events, locales, and conversations from my memories of them. To maintain their anonymity in some instances, I have changed the names of individuals and places. I may have changed some identifying characteristics and details such as physical properties, occupations, and places of residence.

Shirley Ann Smolko has no responsibility for the persistence or accuracy of URLs for external or third-party Internet Websites referred to in this publication and does not guarantee that any content on such Websites is, or will remain, accurate or appropriate.

Designations used by companies to distinguish their products are often claimed as trademarks. All brand names and product names used in this book or on its cover are trademarks of their respective owners. The publishers and the author are not associated with any product or vendor mentioned in this book. None of the companies referenced within the book have endorsed the book.

Shirley Ann Smolko asserts the moral right to be identified as the author of this work.

I dedicate this book to the love of my life, Joe, who also happens to be my husband and editor. His love, encouragement, and tenacious editing skills made this book possible. There was a time in our relationship before we were married when he told me that he didn't believe in the afterlife, that when you're dead, you're dead. He's changed his mind!

CONTENTS

Preface

Reports of haunted hospitals abound in just about every major city in the United States. All you have to do is google "haunted hospitals" and you'll find a plethora of haunted hospitals around the world. My purpose in writing this book is to share my experiences as a psychic while working as a hospital nurse, not necessarily to prove that hospitals are haunted. However, while writing about my work experiences with spirits, I realized even more that hospitals are extremely haunted places.

Ghostly activity may continue in a hospital long after it has been abandoned or demolished. Spirits tend to stay at a location even when the structure is torn down and something else is built. Earthbound spirits who have a high level of conscious awareness can see the changes that have been made in a building. Spirits who have a lower level of conscious awareness and are stuck in time will not see the changes in their space. They will always see the building the way it was when they were alive, even after the structure is long gone.

Negative energy on the site of a demolished hospital is absorbed into the ground and imprinted onto the etheric space of where the hospital structure once existed. When a hospital is torn down, I think a blessing and crossing over ceremony needs to be performed to cleanse the land and space before any other building is constructed in its place. Unfortunately, whenever a hospital is torn down, the demolition manager isn't going to delay the wrecking ball until he can find someone to perform a clearing and blessing. So, the hauntings continue in the space even when a new structure is built.

A prime example of this type of haunting is found in my first book, *Adventures of a Psychic Nurse: Spirits Everywhere!* In the eleventh chapter, I wrote about an evil, earthbound spirit who had been a pedophile when he was alive. Upon his death in prison, the land escheated to the state and the dilapidated house he had lived in was torn down. The land was sold several decades afterward, and a young couple bought the land with the intention of building a new house. The new house was built on the site of the old house—the house this perverted man had occupied before he went to prison, and returned to after he died. I was told the soul of this man had been possessed and was being controlled by a demon called the *The Spirit of Sexual Perversion of the Innocents* (which also happens to be the title of the story). The following is a passage excerpted from that story:

Apparently, he had been arrested and brought to justice for his crimes of pornography involving innocent children. Now, the spirit of this old man was loose in the brand new home of my client and his family. It was up to me to get him out, so they could live in peace without interference from the demon in human form that I referred to as Mr. Pervert.

The morning of the evening of the investigation, I communed with The Great Spirit and commanded its help in the form of its mightiest warrior angel, St. Michael, the Archangel. I communicated my command to God by visualizing St. Michael leading thousands of his warrior angels to do battle against what I perceived as the Spirit of Sexual Perversion of the Innocents. I continued to watch while my creative visualization morphed into an observation. At that point I knew God was manifesting the outcome I was seeking. The angels took hold of the evil Spirit binding it with rope while freeing the human soul it had possessed. I continued to watch as the angels escorted the old man into the light of The Creator and the evil possessing spirit into the black abyss.

A month after the cleansing and blessing, I gave the couple a follow-up call. Everything was quiet, and they hadn't experienced anymore paranormal activity.

The lost souls that haunt hospitals may be confused, have unfinished business, are afraid of what awaits them on the other side, or are hungry for physical life and looking for someone they can easily possess to fulfill their fleshy desires. Regardless of the reason for their choice to remain earthbound, ghosts can be found in every corridor and room inside a hospital. Hospitals are very haunted, and I should know because I am a psychic nurse. Join me on my adventures into the fascinating world of spirits and haunted hospitals!

~ One ~

POSSESSED PATIENTS

"There are no experts. You probably know more about possession than most priests. Look, your daughter doesn't say she's a demon; she says he's the devil himself. Now, if you've seen as many psychotics as I have, you'd say it's the same thing as saying you're Napoleon Bonaparte. You asked me, what I think is best for your daughter. Six months...under observation...at the best hospital you can find."

— Father Damien Karras, *The Exorcist*

Possession or Mental Illness?

Early in my nursing career, I worked part-time at a private psychiatric hospital. This hospital had four units. Unit one treated patients with drug and alcohol addictions. Unit two treated adult patients with acute psychiatric disorders. Unit three treated patients with chronic psychiatric disorders, and unit four treated pediatric patients with acute and chronic psychiatric disorders. Working as a psychiatric nurse was new to me. I had worked only as a medical-surgical nurse up to that point in my career. I was usually assigned to units one and two, but on this particular day I was asked to work unit four with the pediatric patients. I initially protested stating that I didn't feel I had enough experience to work with the pediatric patients. My supervisor told me I was hired to work all the units and I was the best choice and more than qualified to work with the children. Although I may have been more than qualified, I definitely was not prepared for what would transpire during that eight hour shift. Before I describe the shocking events of that day, I need to explain what I feel are the somewhat subtle differences between mental illness and demonic possession.

To the secular mental healthcare worker, there is no such thing as demonic possession. Upon assessment by a psychiatrist, violent psychiatric patients are given a DSM 5 diagnosis, or diagnoses, that most closely describes their behavioral characteristics and presenting symptoms. The *DSM* or the *Diagnostic and Statistical Manual of Mental Disorders* is a publication for the classification of mental disorders using a common language and standard criteria. The most current edition is the *DSM 5* published in 2013. There are no criteria in this manual to help distinguish between pure mental illness and demonic possession. However, possession and possession trance are now listed under the diagnosis "dissociative disorder not otherwise specified." The DSM-IV-TR defines *possession trance* as: "a single or episodic alteration in the state of consciousness characterized by the replacement of customary sense of personal identity by a new identity, which is attributed to the influence of a spirit, power, or deity."

To differentiate between mental illness and demonic possession, it is necessary to rule out ordinary mental illness. Some clergy believe possession may be the cause of mental illnesses that cannot be explained through one of five clusters of causal attributes. According to King, Leavey, & Lowenthal (2016) the causal attributions for mental illness are grouped into five main clusters or dimensions as follows:

(1) Biomedical attributions such as brain chemistry imbalance, brain damage and organic problems related to alcohol and drug use.

(2) Personal life events, which affect individuals across all social classes (although there may be a social class effect related to incidence, impact and outcome). This category includes causal attributes such as bereavement, relationship problems, work stress, and isolation.

(3) Conditions at a social level, which include common socio-economic deficits such as poverty, unemployment, poor housing, migration, racism, and discrimination.

(4) Modernity, which includes problems associated with modern living and is closely related to materialism. This category, therefore, includes attributes such as secularism and loss of religious identity.

(5) Religious and supernatural attributes, which includes non-natural causes of mental illness such as de-

monic possession or oppression, witchcraft, and engagement with the occult.

Clergy commonly suggest close causal links between different attributes. For example, a supernatural explanation of illness may suggest that an individual's lifestyle, socio-economic circumstances, or personal tragedy may leave them vulnerable to supernatural or demonic exploitation. In other instances, mental illness itself can lead to oppression or demonic possession.

To distinguish between ordinary mental illness and demonic possession, it is necessary to assess for specific signs indicative of possession. According to Dr. Richard Gallagher, MD (2016) a possessed individual may demonstrate the following signs:

> A possessed individual may suddenly, in a type of trance, voice statements of astonishing venom and contempt for religion, while understanding and speaking various foreign languages previously unknown to them. The subject might also exhibit enormous strength or even the extraordinarily rare phenomenon of levitation. [I have not witnessed a levitation myself, but half a dozen people I work with vow that they've seen it in the course of their exorcisms.] He or she might demonstrate "hidden knowledge" of all sorts of things—like how a stranger's loved ones died, what secret sins she has committed, even where people are at a given moment. These are skills that cannot be explained except by special psychic or preternatural ability.

It is apparent from Dr. Gallagher's description that possession may be determined by the existence of preternatural ability or paranormal phenomenon in the victim. In addition to levitation mentioned above, cases of possession have been reported where the victims exhibited the paranormal ability to move objects with their minds and use them as missiles to harm or intimidate others. Possessed patients may have none, some, or all of the causal attributions of mental illness present. Demonic possession can occur first and produce the symptoms of mental illness, or it can occur due to an individual's vulnerability because of mental illness.

Exorcists use certain tricks of the trade to trigger paranormal phenomenon when called in to investigate a possible possession. Of course, a patient with classic textbook mental illness will not exhibit any paranormal abilities when triggered by a stimulus while a possessed patient will. Some of the tricks an exorcist may use to look for signs of possession or trigger paranormal activity in the possessed are:

1. The exorcist covertly gives the patient holy water to drink instead of regular water while watching for a reaction such as choking, coughing, vomiting, or paranormal activity.
2. The exorcist dowses his hands with holy water, holy oil, or blessed salt before greeting the patient and offering a handshake, which is either refused or the patient reacts violently or exhibits para-

normal phenomenon upon contact with the hand of the exorcist.

3. The exorcist carries a holy object such as a cross or holy medallion, which is hidden on the exorcist or in plain view. Even if the object is hidden, the possessed patient will react negatively showing signs of irritation, aggression, or paranormal phenomenon.

4. The exorcist prays for the patient, which elicits irritability, profanity, aggressive behavior, and ultimately paranormal phenomenon in the individual.

Individuals with classic textbook psychiatric disorders will not exhibit any of the above noted paranormal signs. They will exhibit symptoms found within the *Diagnostic Manual of Psychiatric Disorders* or *DSM*. The possessed individual may exhibit symptoms of mental illness in addition to some or all of the above noted paranormal signs. The defining criteria in determining a true possession includes some or all of the paranormal signs noted above. As you will see, the patient anecdotes in this chapter all meet the criteria for possession.

Monster Man

I started my workday by getting report from the night nurse, which didn't include anything out of the ordinary for this patient population. Three of the four patients I was receiving that morning had emotional disorders and were stable. The fourth patient had just been admitted to our unit from the E.D. His admission assessment had not been completed and the only item noted was that this psychotic nine-year-old boy had been brought to the hospital around two o'clock in the morning by his affluent parents. I would have to research this patient's E.D. record and any prior psychiatric history, evaluate him, and then perform his admission assessment.

I checked on my patients after receiving report. My stable patients were already up and dressing for breakfast. My new patient was sitting calmly on the floor in the middle of the padded room. His straight jacket had been removed and a mental health tech had been assigned to watch him from a chair at the entrance to the padded room per the psychiatrist's orders. After breakfast I started my morning assessments, which involved an open ended question and answer segment followed by therapeutic conversation on each patient.

I completed assessments on all three of my stable patients saving the new admission, whom I'll refer to as Dale, for last. My assessments took no more than fifteen minutes and were uneventful for each of my stable patients. That, however, would not be the case with my new admit who was still calm and sitting in the middle of the floor in the padded room at ten o'clock that morning when I walked in to do his assessment.

As soon as I crossed the threshold of the door, this young child screamed out in agony as if he were being tortured and commanded me to get rid of my earrings. I told him that I liked my earrings and I wasn't going to get rid of them.

He replied, "I know all about those earrings. You got them from that church full of hypocrites. All of you are sinners and you're going to hell. Awe, you're such a good Sunday School teacher, aren't you?"

I promptly took the earrings out of my ears and placed them in the left pocket of my white uniform top. The mental health aide and I were able to quickly de-escalate the situation by telling Dale that the earrings were put away and that we would have to put the straight jacket back on him if he couldn't calm down because we didn't want him to hurt himself or us. In a low voice, he pleaded with us not to put the straight jacket on him by saying that he would calm down. I told him I needed to do his admission assessment and asked him if he would be able to cooperate. He said he would and promised to remain calm. I took a couple of deep breaths and began the assessment interview. I asked Dale why he reacted to my earrings the way he did. After a few moments of silence, he said to me in a low gravelly voice, "I just don't like them. Okay."

The only jewelry the staff was allowed to wear were post earrings. For obvious reasons, dangling jewelry such as necklaces and bracelets were not allowed because a patient could grab this jewelry and use it to hold and harm a staff member. On this particular day I decided to wear my silver cross post earrings, which had been a gift of appreciation from my church for teaching the toddler Sunday School class every other Sunday. I alternated teaching this class with another teacher, which worked out perfectly for both of us since we were both nurses and were obligated to work for our respective hospital employers every other weekend. I had no idea when I put those earrings on that morning the effect they would have on my new admission. How could he have known they were a gift from my church?

I continued the interview portion of the assessment by asking Dale why he came to the hospital. I was definitely not prepared for what he told me. "I tried to kill my parents and sister with a knife." I read in his ED record that his parents had brought him to the hospital in the middle of the night because he was behaving aggressively, but nowhere was it noted that he tried to kill his family.

I asked him why he would try to kill them.

He said, "Because, the demon told me to do it. He said he would kill me in my sleep and take me to hell if I didn't kill my family."

Then I asked him if this demon had a name and what it looked like.

His reply was, "I can't say his real name because he will come to me. I call it 'Monster Man'. He has big black eyes, a long skinny face, jagged teeth, pointed ears, two horns on its head, his fingers are long and sharp and he has hoofs instead of feet."

I allowed a minute of silence before continuing with the interview, more out of a need to digest what I had just heard than out of an attempt to provide therapeutic communication. What this nine year old had just told me chilled me to the bone. I knew that Dale was telling the truth. I knew he wasn't experiencing a delusion because I could feel the evil demon he had just described lurking in the shadows. I could hear monster man laughing and saying, "You can't help him. Nobody can. He's mine!"

I asked Dale how he was feeling now and if he still wanted to kill his family.

He said: "I feel okay now and I don't want to kill my family. I love them. Whenever I tell monster man that I won't hurt my family, he chokes me and throws me around. Then I become angry and he takes control of my body and makes me do things that I don't want to do."

Next, I asked him why he let monster man make him do things he doesn't want to do.

He said: "I'm outside my body and he's inside. It's like I'm watching monster man do things I don't like through me and I can't make him stop. He takes total control and won't listen to me. Sometimes he does things that I don't remember him doing, and I get blamed for it."

I observed Dale becoming increasingly agitated and thought it would best to end the interview. I thanked Dale for being open and honest, and I asked him to let a staff member know when monster man was bothering him.

In a low gravelly voice that didn't sound like his own, he said, "I'll bother him whenever I want to and if you try to interfere, I'll bother you too!"

I didn't respond to the threat. I glanced over at the mental health aide who had a look of shock and disbelief written all over his face. This mental health aide was assigned to be one-on-one with Dale for the rest of the shift to monitor his behavior and look for signs of escalation. I patted the aide on the shoulder as I turned and walked out the door of the padded room. Fortunately, Dale remained relatively calm for the remainder of the shift, which was good because I had another admission that afternoon who would prove to be much more of a challenge than my morning admission with Dale or any other psychiatric admission I had ever had.

The Devil Did It!

A t noon I received report on my new patient, Seth. The report I received from the emergency department nurse was that he had been brought to the hospital in the early morning hours by his parents who reported they woke up to find their son butchering their cat in the middle of the kitchen floor. They said he appeared to be in a trance and would not respond to any of them. He just kept cutting their beloved pet into pieces. His father was able to remove the knife from his son's hand without a struggle. Seth remained in a trance-like state until they reached the entrance to the emergency department.

As soon as they entered through the automatic doors, he started kicking, screaming and asking why they were at the hospital. His parents explained to him that he needed help because he had killed their cat. He said, "I didn't do it! The devil did it! I saw him do it. Please, it wasn't me!"

Their teenage daughter, Dana, also witnessed the event and became hysterical. She exhibited signs of debilitating shock and will probably have to receive counseling for a long time. The E.D. nurse said he would be sending Seth to the unit around one o'clock, so I decided to go ahead and take a lunch break. As I ate my lunch of leftover lasagna and garlic bread in the staff break room, my mind returned to the interview I had with Dale earlier that morning. I wondered how anything as heinous as a nine year old trying to kill his family could be possible. Was Dale homicidal and trying to avoid accountability for his actions or was he really possessed by monster man? A part of me had a difficult time believing what Dale had said to me, but I knew deep in my heart that something truly evil dwelled deep inside of him.

I have always had the ability to discern spirits, both good and evil just by feeling their presence and I could not deny what I perceived. Up to that point, monster man was the most evil presence I had ever encountered, which would change when I admitted my next patient, Seth.

I took fifteen minutes for lunch instead of the usual thirty minutes to have plenty of time to prepare to receive my new patient from the E.D. as scheduled at one o'clock. When I walked back onto the unit, however, I was informed by the charge nurse that the E.D. had to go ahead and move the patient to the unit because they had received more patients who needed to be triaged. She told me he was waiting for me in the second padded room with a mental health aide assigned to do one-on-one observation, and I could do my admission assessment anytime. He no longer had a straight jacket on because he had been given a tranquilizer and a sedative in the E.D. and was now calm.

I checked on my other patients before heading over to the padded room to complete my assessment on Seth.

From the hallway, I could see he was sitting on the floor and his 6'3", 275 lb. mental health aide, Jamal, was standing just inside the entrance to the door. The moment I walked into the padded room, Seth lunged at me, screaming, "I'll kill you, church lady. Get rid of those damn earrings now!" I remembered that I had put those earrings into the left pocket of my uniform top when Dale also screamed at me to get rid of them. I thought to myself, *How could he know? What are the odds of having two patients admitted on the same day who are possessed by demons?*

Jamal sprung into action to restrain this violent 5'4', 135 lb. twelve-year-old boy to no avail. Seth picked up Jamal and threw him against the wall as if he were nothing more than a rag doll. I yelled out for help and pressed the safety code button just outside the entrance of the door. Within a few seconds I had at least ten people in the room with me to take Seth down. Our resident psychiatrist, Dr. Giovanni, was also on the unit and responded to the code. It took everyone in the room to subdue Seth and safely tackle him face down to the floor. He was now speaking in a foreign language. Dr. Giovanni said that Seth was speaking fluent latin and asked if Seth had formally taken latin. No one knew.

Dr. Giovanni gave me a verbal order to give Ativan 2mg IM stat! I ran to the med-room, drew up the medication into a syringe and was back into the padded room within what seemed like fifteen seconds. With Seth struggling and trying to throw everyone off of him, I managed to inject the thick viscous medication into his left hip. He continued to thrash and fight for several minutes before the medication started to take effect and he began to relax. We managed to get the straight jacket on him before releasing our strong hold and closing the door to the padded room.

Jamal was sent to the E.D. to be assessed for any injuries he may have sustained by being thrown against the wall. We assigned a new mental health aide, Alex, to observe Seth through the port hole outside the closed door. It is necessary to monitor any patient that has been given a tranquilizer for respiratory depression and the inability to handle oral secretions, especially when they have also been physically restrained.

After a quick and informal debriefing with the staff, I returned to the nurses' station, along with Dr. Giovanni who called Seth's parents to let them know we had to tranquilize and restrain their son because of his psychotic episode. While he was on the phone, I overheard the doctor ask Seth's parents if he had ever studied Latin. I then heard the doctor say, "Really, because he was speaking Latin fluently during his episode."

When Dr. Giovanni hung up, he looked at me and said, "He's never had any instruction in Latin. I am going to write some new orders. I'll increase his dose of Thorazine and add Haloperidol p.r.n. (as needed) for increased agitation. Let me know if he gets worse." He didn't make any further comments about the patient's demonstration of xenolalia (the ability to speak in a language, which the individual has not learned). The doctor left the unit immediately after writing the new orders. Although Dr. Giovanni never mentioned the word possession, I have often wondered if that was exactly what he was thinking might be occurring with this patient.

The tranquilizer we gave Seth did not have the complete desired effect we hoped it would. He continued to thrash about, flinging his legs in the air and exhibiting xenolalia. This behavior persisted for at least an hour before Alex yelled out, "He's in the air, he's three feet in the frigging air, he's levitating!" Every available staff member ran to the to the door to see what was happening, but by the time they arrived, Seth had returned to the floor. With a look of shock and disbelief on his face, Alex said, "I swear, he was in the air! I know what I saw. Man, I'm quitting this job!"

After the levitating incident, Seth became calm and fell asleep for the rest of the shift. Dale was also calm and spent his time coloring and drawing pictures. I was never happier to see my relief nurse. I filled her in on all details of what transpired during that day. She said, "Oh my God. I knew I should have called out sick. I just knew it!"

I love children. I have always enjoyed interacting with them. The personalities controlling Dale and Seth I experienced that day were definitely not children. I felt helpless to provide any real therapy because I knew their problems weren't just related to mental illness. What good could I be to them if I couldn't give them the help I felt they really needed, which was spiritual help. I already had a full time job on the Medical-Surgical unit of a nearby Medical Center. I didn't feel that I would be able to handle too many days like this one, so I turned in my two week notice to this private psychiatric hospital the next day. I felt that

I might be better suited for the medical side of nursing. However, I would soon learn that possessed patients are not limited to psychiatric hospitals. Because of new trends in mental healthcare delivery at that time, psychiatric patients were quickly becoming more and more assimilated into the general hospital patient population.

The Witch

B etween 1972 and 1990 14 out of out of 277 state psychiatric hospitals in the U.S. closed due to changing trends in treatment regimens and government policy, as well as the reallocation of state and federal resources. Between 1990 and 2000, 44 of the remaining 263 psychiatric hospitals closed due to lack of state and federal funding. As a result, many mentally ill patients were thrown onto the streets to become homeless, or end up in jail or prison.

A large number of these mentally ill homeless individuals frequently end up in the E.D. of the local general hospital to receive treatment for their acute psychotic episodes. Once they are stabilized in the E.D., they are usually admitted to an inpatient unit for treatment of a physical malady in addition to their psychiatric diagnosis. When I resigned from the private psychiatric hospital where I had been employed part-time, I had no idea I would find myself routinely caring for severely disturbed psychiatric patients in the general medical and surgical patient population of the hospital and trauma center where I worked.

I was working on the cardiac step-down unit of a large medical center when I encountered Wendy Willis—The

Witch. Wendy was a petite 62 year old lady who was 4'9" tall and weighed approximately 88 pounds. She looked much older than her age. She had deep wrinkles on her forehead, around her mouth, and eyes. Her hair was shoulder length, gray, and stringy. She had blue-green eyes, and an aquiline nose. Her smile was more like a grimace, resembling a jack-o-lantern missing every other tooth.

She had been admitted to our unit the day before with a cardiac arrhythmia and was scheduled for pacemaker surgery the next day. We usually didn't accept general cardiac surgery patients patients on the cardiac step-down unit. Our core patient population consisted of open heart and carotid endarterectomy surgical patients who had been discharged from the CCU. My understanding was that she was on our unit because the cardiac unit was full and we were getting the overflow.

The report I received on Wendy Willis that morning from the night nurse was that she was experiencing bradycardia (a resting heart rate below 60 beats per minute) in the 30's with symptoms of syncope (fainting) upon ambulation. Her heart rate was still in the 30's and she was now asymptomatic on bedrest. She had no family and was living in a homeless shelter. She had a restful and uneventful night. The doctor had talked to her about her upcoming pacemaker surgery, but she still needed some pre-op teaching on what to expect, and the consent needed to be signed.

After knocking on the partially opened door and announcing my presence, I walked into Wendy's room that morning to do her assessment. The room was freezing to the point where I could see my breath, even though it was summertime and the air conditioning was on throughout the hospital. I looked at the thermostat on the wall as I walked in and noticed that it was set at 76 degrees Fahrenheit, but it felt more like 36 degrees. I made a mental note to have the secretary call maintenance. Despite the closed curtains, enough light peaked through the crack that I could make out the outlines of the furniture in the room. I looked over towards the bed and saw the silhouette of my patient sitting up in the middle of the bed with her legs crossed as if she were meditating.

I walked in a little further in and flipped on the light switch. In the light I could see that her gray hair was completely covering her face. She reminded me of the character "Cousin It" on the *Addams Family* sitcom from the 1960's. As I got closer, I could hear her whispering and repeating some type of mantra that sounded eerie to me. I couldn't make out the words because they weren't from any language I knew. I called out her name and she instantly became quiet.

I told her I wanted to open her draperies to let some sunlight in because sunlight kills germs. She didn't respond, so I walked over to the window and opened the draperies. When I turned around to face her, I was startled to see that she had pulled her hair behind her ears and was glaring at me with her jack-o-lantern looking grin. What she said to me in a gravelly and sarcastic tone of voice made me shudder.

Well, well, look what the devil sent me. It's a holy angel of healing. Aren't you precious. How was choir practice last night? Oh, that's right, your sainted choir director had a stroke. That's so tragic.

I could not believe what I was hearing. How could she know my choir director had a stroke during choir practice. I hadn't told anyone at work. I pretended to ignore her comments with a stoic face and told her I needed to listen to her heart. She said I could do whatever I needed to do. While I auscultated her chest for heart and lung sounds, I heard what sounded like a continuous low pitched growl. It wasn't an adventitious lung sound I was hearing nor was it a heart murmur. Her heart was slow but regular with no extra heart sounds noted. I finished up with the rest of my assessment, tidied up her room, and asked her if there was anything she needed before heading out of the room. She grinned at me once again and said, "No. I don't need anything right now. I'll think about it and let you know later."

As I walked towards the nurses' station, I couldn't wrap my head around what had just transpired. I was filled with an overwhelming sense of dread at the prospect of having to deal with the evil entity who was possessing my patient for the rest of my shift. Unlike my own abilities, this patient's psychic ability was definitely not a gift from God, but an ability given to her from something very dark and evil with the intent to do harm and not good. I knew from the moment I entered her room something very evil was present.

My psychic and mediumship gifts have always brought truth, hope, and healing to those people who need it most. The abilities given to people possessed with evil spirits are a mockery of God and His agents here on earth. The Bible is full of stories about the gifts of the Spirit that Jesus, the disciples, and the prophets of the old testament demonstrated. In many instances Jesus demonstrated psychic knowledge including the incident with the woman at the well. He also created many miracles. In I Corinthians 12:1-31, St. Paul discusses the gifts of the Spirit, which are psychic in nature.

The old testament prophet and wonder worker, Elisha, demonstrated psychic ability. He eavesdropped on the King of Syria while he was making war plans against Israel. Since Elisha was in Israel, he had to have accomplished this feat in one of two ways, either through remote viewing or astral projection. Regardless of his methods, Elisha might be the first recorded psychic spy in history to work for the government. The verse that illustrates Elisha's psychic spy activity is written in 2 Kings 6:12: "One of his advisers said, 'No, my master, O king. The prophet Elisha who lives in Israel keeps telling the king of Israel the things you say in your bedroom'."

In modern times, both the U.S. and Russia have perceived the use of psychics as a valuable form of defense. For instance, from 1978 until 1995, the U.S. used a group of psychic spies to monitor the activity of the Russians. This espionage program, which focused on remote viewing, came to be known as the Stargate Project. Stargate was established in response to the Soviet's use of a psychic program. The U.S. no longer uses psychic spies. It's unclear whether or not the Russians still do.

Many thoughts went through my mind as I continued to make my way to the nurses' station. *Why was this patient assigned to me? Am I going to receive a lot of grief from this patient today? Is she going to be disruptive? How I'm I going to get through the shift?* I recognized my own negative self-talk and immediately replaced it with faith-filled Bible verses and Unity affirmations. I also repeated the Unity prayer of protection several times in my head. A sense of peace and calm came upon me, and I knew I had power over this evil entity. Any plans it had to torment me that day would be foiled.

An hour had passed and I was pleased that Ms. Willis had not displayed any disruptive behavior. As soon as I finished my assessments, I started the med pass. I planned to medicate the more critical open heart patients first, saving Ms. Willis for last. Although I had anticipated trouble from Ms. Willis during the med pass, I was able to administer meds to my other patients without any interruptions from her. After all of my other patients were medicated, I made my way to Ms. Willis's room with her medication.

She was awake and sitting up in the recliner when I knocked and entered the room.

She looked over at me and said, "It's the angel of healing the devil sent me. What kind of poison did you bring me?"

I told her that I didn't have any poison, just the Aminophyline the doctor prescribed for her bradycardia.

In a sardonic tone of voice she replied, "Oh, isn't that nice. He wants to fix my heart."

I handed her the medication along with some fresh water. She took it, tossed it into her mouth, and swallowed it with a few sips of water. I asked her if there was anything I could do for her before I left the room and she replied:

Yes, My Dear, there is something you can do for me—stop praying! I know you prayed against me. Don't do it anymore! If you do, I have no other alternative but to curse and torment you! I am a witch and I know how to cast spells. I do the devil's bidding and he gives me great power.

I told her I was there to provide nursing care and nothing more. I also told her that I would continue to pray anytime I felt compelled to and I wasn't afraid of her threats because I was protected. I went on to say I knew she was planning on tormenting me by creating chaos on the unit. I also told her any chaos she created would risk the safety and well being of my other patients, and I wasn't about to let her do that. She hissed at me and starting speaking what sounded like latin. I told her I would check on her later. Then I turned and walked out of the room.

One hour later, I was removing a chest tube from an open heart patient when I received a stat page to Ms. Willis's room. I quickly finished up the procedure and ran across the foyer to her room. On the way over I knew she was creating some type of mischief, and I resented being called to her room because of her shenanigans. When I entered the room, two CNAs were there trying to figure out a way to get her off of the floor. She was on her belly slithering around like a snake with her tongue thrusting in and out of her mouth while she made hissing sounds. Her pupils took on the elliptical appearance of a snake. They were dilated and black, taking up almost the whole sclera (white surface) of her eye. She wouldn't let anyone touch her and tried to bite anyone who came close enough.

I attempted to reason with her by telling her she shouldn't be up because the strain of activity on her heart could cause her to go into complete heart failure, which might lead to death. She didn't reply or even acknowledge me. She just continued to writhe around on her belly. I knew we needed help if we were going to safely get her off the floor, so I pulled the work mobile phone out of my scrub pocket and tried to dial the unit secretary to get her to call a code gray (security alert). Before I could finish the call, Ms. Willis lunged at me, grabbed my leg and tried to bite me. Fortunately, I was able to quickly pull away from her. I ran outside the room and completed my call to the secretary asking her to call a code gray to room 606. From the door, I asked one of the two CNAs to press the nurse call button and ask for the charge nurse to come to the room stat and bring four point restraints.

Within what seemed like a matter of seconds, four burley security guards were in the room. They gently but swiftly lifted Ms. Willis off the floor and put her back into the bed. At the same time, the nurse supervisor ran in with the four point restraints and in the presence of security, we placed the restraints on her. She thrashed and contorted her body while spewing profanities and spitting on us the whole time we were putting restraints on her. We didn't let her behavior distract us. We quickly and efficiently applied the restraints while trying to dodge direct hits of her spit to our faces. Once the restraints were on, she said in a low, gravelly and hissing voice, "You'll all pay for binding me up. I will curse all of you! You will suffer greatly for what you have done!" Because of the seriousness of her heart condition, we assigned a CNA to sit with Ms. Willis to monitor her for physical duress.

Shortly after we restrained her, she lapsed into a trance-like state of consciousness and started speaking in unknown tongues. She ignored any attempts of communication from the staff and wouldn't acknowledge the presence of anyone in the room. Ironically, she remained asymptomatic with her heart rate in the 30's throughout the whole psychotic episode and thereafter. She didn't experience any shortness of breath, fainting, or weakness. Her blood pressure and other vital signs remained in her baseline range. She continued in a trance-like state of consciousness, exhibiting glossolalia until about six that evening at which time she became silent and catatonic as evidenced by her body rigidity and resistance to repositioning.

Whenever a patient is restrained, every two hours they must have their restraints released and reapplied. In addition they must be repositioned and offered nourishment and fluids. Her restraints were released and reapplied one restraint at a time, but she was so rigid and resistant to being moved that she couldn't be repositioned. Along with several other staff members we tried to reposition her, but it was futile. She might as well have weighed a ton because we could not turn her—she was completely catatonic at this point.

Thirty minutes later, my relief nurse showed up for report. I was so happy to be ending this shift. I was scheduled to be off the next couple of days for which I was extremely grateful. I didn't feel I would be able to tolerate another bizarre day. I gave the night nurse report on all of my patients and clocked out as quickly as possible.

That night as I lay in bed, I prayed that Ms. Willis would be released from the grip of whatever evil had controlled her and that she would have a successful and uneventful surgery, which would bring her healing. Three days later when I returned to work, I asked the charge nurse about Ms. Willis and was told she came out of her catatonic state of consciousness the night before her procedure (which was the night that I had prayed for her). Her surgery the next day was successful, and she was discharged to a nursing home the day after. Although whatever was controlling Ms. Willis tried to put me through hell, I was relieved to hear that she had a good outcome. There's no doubt in my mind that in addition to being mentally ill, Ms. Willis was definitely possessed by something extremely sinister. I believe it continually tormented her and tried to torment others through her as well.

~ Two ~

HAUNTED HOSPITAL WINGS

"Ghosts are all around us. Look for them, and you will find them"

—Ruskin Bond

The Ghosts of Dix Hill

I did a clinical rotation on the medical-surgical unit of a psychiatric hospital in Raleigh, N.C. called Dorothea Dix Hospital, notoriously known as "Dix Hill." Before I tell you the story about my experience with the haunted wing at this hospital, which had been closed due to electrical issues and unexplained activity, I'd like to give you the fascinating history of this spooky insane asylum.

In 1848, when Dorothea Lynde Dix, nurse and social reformer, toured the state, she discovered that the mentally ill were incarcerated in jails and stuck in poorhouses where they were being horribly mistreated. Appalled by what she had witnessed, she addressed the N.C. legislature with her concerns about how the mentally ill were being treated. She was able to persuade the lawmakers and gained approval for funds to be set aside to build the state's first psychiatric hospital. By 1851 a tract of 182 acres on the outskirts of town, west of Raleigh, had been acquired, and planning for the Dix facility was begun. The first building constructed was a Romanesque structure with a large central section and two wings. A second building, containing a kitchen, bakery, and apartments for staff, was soon added. These two buildings were the first public buildings in Raleigh to have steam heat and gas lighting.

The hospital was completed and began admitting patients in 1856. Dix recommended light work and exercise for the mentally ill who had previously been confined, and she sent them Bibles, prayer books, and pictures. Over the years, its mental heath services expanded and additional buildings were constructed. In 1902 the Dorothea Dix School of Nursing was established. By the mid-twentieth century, the hospital occupied 1,248 acres, much of them left as forest. In 1959 the name of the facility was changed to Dorothea Dix Hospital, in memory of the woman who had been essential to its founding. Ironically, when the hospital was built, Dorothea Dix refused to have the hospital named after her but agreed to the designation of the site on which it was located as "Dix Hill," in memory of her physician grandfather, Elijah Dix.

By 1974 the Dix complex had grown to 282 buildings on 2,354 acres, plus 1,300 acres of farmland; patient capacity was 2,756. Over the next several decades, demand for long-term hospitalization for the mentally ill declined as out-patient care was emphasized. In addition, other state hospitals and private institutions offered mental health services that were closer and more convenient for many citizens. By the early 2000's, Dix Hospital had 120 buildings and occupied a 425-acre tract, accommodating a maximum of 682 patients. The hospital's approximately $60 million annual budget was supported by state and federal funds as well as patient fees. In August 2012, due to lack of state and federal funding, Dorothea Dix Hospital permanently closed its doors. The last patients were moved to Central Regional Hospital in Butner, N.C., which did not provide enough beds for even the most serious cases.

On the day of my experience with the haunted wing, I was assigned a schizophrenic patient with advanced tertiary syphilis who was diagnosed with dementia secondary to neurosyphilis. Syphilis is caused by the bacterial spirochete, treponema pallidum, which is curable with antibiotics; however, damage to organs and other tissues is not reversible if antibiotic treatment is not received in a timely manner. Unfortunately, my patient never received antibiotic treatment soon enough to stop the dissemination of the infection.

She was covered with gummas on her chest, abdomen, legs and arms. A gumma is a solitary granulomatous lesion with central necrosis, or dead tissue. They typically occur on the skin or bone but can be found anywhere. These lesions may affect any organ system but most commonly occur in the skin, mucous membranes, and bones. Tertiary or late syphilis is classified into gummatous syphilis, cardiovascular syphilis, and neurosyphilis.

The doctor wrote a stat order for a new treatment on my patient that included Silvadene cream to be applied to her lesions B.I.D., which is twice a day. Silvadene Sulfonamide is a topical antimicrobial drug used on the skin to prevent or treat serious infections. I wanted to keep the sheets off of her body to avoid irritation to the gummas and keep the silvadene from being rubbed off, so I decided a bed cradle would do the job. However, the bed cradle I wanted was stored in a closed wing on the other side of the hospital. I needed to implement this treatment quickly because it was ordered stat; however, the central supply person for our unit was at lunch and wouldn't be able to get it for me. The charge nurse, Mrs. Crocker, told me that I would have to go to another wing and get a bed cradle out of storage myself. She said I needed to take a couple of other students with me because I shouldn't go alone.

I had no problem getting a couple of my fellow students, Betty and Mary, to go with me. They were excited at the prospect of touring a different part of the hospital. The charge nurse gave me a big ring of keys and we were on our way. The three of us had to pass through a series of several units, unlocking and locking doors between the units as we went. The scenes we witnessed on some of these units were shocking, but we didn't let that slow us down. If anything, we were more in a hurry to pass through. It was not unusual to see some of these patients openly pleasuring themselves until they were redirected by staff members. We also witnessed several patients pacing the floor and a few of others dancing around in circles.

It seemed to take forever before we reached the north wing of the hospital where the bed cradle was stored.

We were astonished at what we saw when we opened the door to the storage unit of the north wing. It was as if we had stepped back in time. There were rusty old metal frame beds and several types of old wheelchairs. Some of these wheelchairs had a wicker back and seat, with leg and foot rests made of solid wood and metal wheels. Others had an upholstered back and seat with a foot rest made of solid wood but no leg rests. A couple looked like rocking chairs without the rockers. Instead, they had metal wheels with solid wood foot rests and no leg rests. There were several metal gurneys with large wheels. Against the wall to the right was what looked like an iron lung.

Farther in, we saw the bed cradles stacked up on a long wooden table to our left. As I walked over to get the bed cradle, I heard a cat call whistle and a felt a tug on the back hem of my dress uniform. With my back towards them, I told my cohorts to cut it out. They asked me what I was talking about. I told them to stop whistling and pulling on my dress. I turned around to look at them and they were still standing by the door. With serious and puzzled looks on their faces, they adamantly denied doing anything.

I grabbed the bed cradle and as I turned around again to join my fellow students, I saw the culprit who had pulled on the hem of my dress. Sitting about five feet away from me in one of the old wicker wheelchairs was a solid looking man. His light brown, shoulder length, stringy hair was disheveled. The menacing grin he had on his face revealed dark brown teeth with noticeable plaque buildup, no doubt from lack of proper oral hygiene as well as chewing tobacco and snuff. He was wearing what looked like a gray confederate uniform with both pant legs folded back and pinned to the pants on the top side of his thighs. In my head, I asked him why he was there.

With a grimace still on his face, he replied, "I'm just waiting to get my new legs. They're making them for me now."

I asked him if he saw a light.

He said, "Look little Miss Prissy, I saw a light a long time ago. I didn't go then and I'm not going now."

He erupted into a devilish cackling laugh that made my skin crawl. I caught up with my cohorts and wasted no time getting back through the door. We barely spoke to one another as we quickly made our way back to the medical-surgical unit.

As soon as we arrived back on the unit, my cohorts asked me what happened in the storage room. They said they saw my dress being pulled up and away from my leg but didn't see that it was caught on anything. They asked me why I accused them of whistling and tugging on my dress. I told them I had heard a cat call whistle followed by a tug on my dress. Then I told them I saw a confederate soldier who looked as if he may have been a below the knee bilateral amputee. I also told them he was waiting for his new legs.

Betty looked at me and laughingly said, "If you're not careful they're gonna lock you up in here with the rest of the crazies."

Mary chimed in and rescued me by saying, "I heard a

whistle too. I also saw your dress being pulled up and away from your leg."

Betty jumped in again and said, "I admit that I was spooked out, but I think our imaginations just got the best of us."

Mary replied, "Spoken like a true psychiatric nurse."

I returned the keys to the charge nurse and asked if anyone had ever experienced anything out of the ordinary in the storage unit. She said there had been many stories over the years of people being touched when they go in there. She told me to go ahead and give my patient her treatment, and then she would meet me in the staff lounge to fill me in on all the strange things that have happened in the hospital over the years.

It took me about fifteen minutes to complete the treatment on my patient before I went directly to the staff lounge and waited for the charge nurse. Mrs. Crocker had worked at the hospital since the late forties and was well respected by the staff as a nurse, leader, and a very knowledgeable hospital historian. She was a tough but caring nurse who carried herself with an air of dignity as evidenced by her starchy white dress uniform, large white cap with two black stripes and sturdy white, laced-up shoes. She was truly a nurse from the old school.

Within a couple of minutes she arrived and sat down at the head of the table beside me. She looked at me with a smile on her face and said, "Tell me what happened in the storage unit. Just about everyone who goes there has a spooky experience." I told her that I heard a cat call whistle and felt a tug on my dress. When I turned around to join my schoolmates, I saw a Civil War soldier sitting in a wicker wheelchair. He looked as if he was a bilateral below-the-knee amputee. I asked him what he was doing there, and he said he was waiting for his legs. I didn't waste anytime getting out of there. Mrs. Crocker chuckled at me and then filled me in on some historical Dix Hill ghost stories:

> I don't think anyone has ever mentioned seeing a ghost in there but there are many female employees who said they were inappropriately touched. Other employees have witnessed objects being moved or thrown while they were in there. I'm not surprised that you saw a Civil War soldier. Soon after the war many veterans came to Dix Hill to be fitted for prosthetic limbs and to be rehabilitated so they could resume earning a living for their families. For many years, the north wing housed only male patients. I believe a lot of these male patients were sexually frustrated when they died and as ghosts they are releasing pent up sexual energy by inappropriately touching the females that go on their wing.

> The portion of the wing that is now being used for storage had to be closed to patient use because of the escalation of unexplainable activity. Lights would flicker on and off. Objects at the nurses station would go missing or move on their own. Several nurses claim to have seen pencils lift out of a cup and go flying through the air like missiles. Cabinet doors would open and slam shut. File cabinet drawers would open with files thrown and scattered all over the floor. Nurses were constantly being groped or touched in a sexually explicit way

while male orderlies were shoved with enough force to push them into a wall or make them fall. You're the only one I know of that actually saw a ghost in the storage unit. However, you wouldn't be the only one to see a ghost in this hospital.

Many employees including me have seen ghosts. This hospital is very haunted. In 1910, there was a lady name Ella who was admitted with a diagnosis of catastrophic schizophrenia. She was also three months pregnant and her mental illness prognosis was very poor. I don't know of anyone with a diagnosis of catastrophic schizophrenia who ever got better. Anyway, six months later she gave birth in the hospital to a healthy baby boy who was sent to an orphanage where he was immediately adopted by a wealthy family. Soon after giving birth, Ella died from failure to thrive. She refused to eat and sobbed unconsolably both day and night. She would pitifully cry out over and over, "The devil took my baby away. Help me get him back." Many employees say they often see her near the entrance to the south wing asking everyone who comes through the door to help her get her baby back. Some people don't see her but hear her pleas to get her baby back.

In 1880 a patient named Marcy was admitted to a unit on the south wing with diagnoses of nymphomania, melancholy, and hysteria. Her husband, Thomas, had her committed with the false allegation that she was having sexual affairs with several different men. It wasn't Marcy that was having affairs, but her husband. He met and fell in love with a much younger woman and wanted to marry her, but before he could do that he had to get rid of his wife. You see, Marcy came from a well-to-do family with great wealth and the only way her husband felt he could gain complete control of her money and business interests was to have her put away. Marcy's father, however, had her husband investigated and found that he was guilty of having several affairs before putting his wife into an asylum.

Marcy's father appeared before a judge with eye witnesses and sworn affidavits attesting to Marcy's stellar behavior as a wife and Thomas's illicit affairs with several women. He was able to prove that Marcy's was falsely accused by her scandalous, lying husband. Witnesses testified that it was Thomas who was unfaithful, not Marcy. Several witnesses said that Thomas was a whoremonger who hung out at the local tavern and took a whore to one of the upstairs bedrooms every night. He was particularly fond of the youngest whore and promised to marry her as soon as he could. The judge found Marcy to be innocent and ordered her release from the asylum into her father's custody. He also granted her a divorce based upon the testimony of the witnesses against her husband for infidelity. A warrant for Thomas's arrest was issued for false testimony against his wife leading to her illegal incarceration. However, she would never leave the asylum.

She tragically committed suicide the morning of the same day the judge ordered her release. Her father didn't tell her he was trying to get her released because he didn't want her to be disappointed if it didn't happen. He had planned to surprise her if and when the judge ordered her discharge. She took a metal spoon from breakfast that morning and slipped it into the sleeve of her dress. She broke the spoon end away from the handle and used the handle to slit her wrists. A couple of hours later, one of the attendants found her slumped over on the floor beside her bed in a puddle of blood. She took her life on the side of the bed that was away from the door so it would be difficult for anyone to see what she was doing. She doesn't like men, so any male orderly who enters her room may experience her wrath. Over the years, several orderlies have reported being hit in the scrotum with enough force to put them on the floor in excruciating pain. Others have reported being pushed, tripped, or slapped in the face by an invisible presence.

Marcy's ghostly attacks and appearances are not limited to her room. Orderlies in different units of south wing have reported similar attacks. Most of these male employees reported seeing a lady in 1880's clothing with blood pouring out of her wrists roaming the halls of south wing just before they were attacked. Employees who know Marcy's story believe that it's her ghost that is roaming the halls looking for her next male victim. To this day, the ghost of Marcy continues to haunt all of south hall.

The rest of my clinical rotation at Dix Hospital was uneventful as far as the paranormal goes; however, I could still feel the presence of lost souls roaming the hospital halls. I learned a lot about delivering competent and compassionate care to the mentally ill that semester. The dedicated medical-surgical psychiatric nurses who mentored me during this clinical experience demonstrated what it takes to provide excellent care. Several of these nurses told me they believed they had a calling from God to care for the mentally ill, and their dedication was obvious by the kindness they showed their patients. This attitude of kindness was not limited to the nurses—the whole staff, including orderlies and nursing assistants, were all very kind.

Ghost Children Still Play There

The Administration at a large hospital where I worked as a cardiac nurse decided to add more hospital beds to our unit to meet the ever increasing demand for cardiac beds. To accomplish this, they closed down the pediatric wing and made it a telemetry unit. The pediatric unit, which had been on the east wing for over forty years, was moved to a shorter wing on one of the other floors. The large waiting area, which divided the two units, was reconstructed to join the two units together making it one wing. Once the old pediatric unit was remodeled and the telemetry monitors were installed, we started admitting heart patients. Shortly thereafter every bed on the remodeled section of the wing was filled. There was absolutely no sign it had once been a pediatric unit. The cute murals and wallpaper, which peppered the walls, were completely removed or covered up with fresh paint.

We had occupied the wing for only a little over a month when patients, visitors, and staff reported seeing children playing on the unit. I walked into Mr. Smith's room one morning to do his a.m. assessment and give him his morning meds. Mr. Smith, a 76-year-old man, was scheduled to have a cardiac catheterization that day. He looked over at me with a smile on his face as I knocked on his door and entered his room. I introduced myself and told him that I would be his nurse until 7 p.m. that evening. When I asked him how he slept the night before, he replied:

> I slept soundly, but when I opened my eyes this morning, there were two little girls, about five or six years old, standing beside my bed. They asked me if I wanted to play hide-and-go-seek with them. Of course, I told them that I couldn't because I wasn't feeling well. They wouldn't take no for an answer and started pulling on my arms and legs. I told them they weren't being very nice and to please leave me alone. They giggled and ran out the door and I haven't seen them since. I thought children under the age of fourteen weren't allowed to be in the patient care areas. If you see their parents, please tell them they need to watch their children more closely. I love children, but they shouldn't be playing in patient rooms. The patients on this unit are sick, including myself.

I told Mr. Smith that if I saw their parents, I would let them know young children are not allowed on the units.

Towards the end of the shift, I told several other staff members about my patient's complaint, and they all denied seeing any children on the unit that day. I didn't see any flesh and blood children, but I did see several ghost children darting in and out of patient rooms throughout the day. These littles one ranged in age from about two to seven years. They were all dressed in cute hospital gowns with little animals or cartoon characters printed on the fabric. Telepathically, I told these ghost children they could stay and play among themselves for now, but not to disturb the grown-up patients who were very sick. They stopped, looked at me, giggled and continued to run and play. Apparently they were not going to listen to me!

A few days after my patient's experience, I was at the nurses's station when a visitor came to the desk to report the children who were alone in the waiting room without supervision. He said he thought small children weren't allowed upstairs and just wanted to let someone know because they were being a little rowdy. As I listened to his complaint, I realized that our freshly painted and remodeled waiting room was a playroom when it was the pediatric unit. I walked down to the the waiting room and found no one there except for the ghost children. As soon as I stuck my head in the door, they all ducked behind chairs and started giggling. I told them if they wanted to stay and play with each other, they would have to behave and not to show themselves to the visitors. I also told them if they didn't behave, I would have to call the angels to take them to heaven. In response to this comment, I received an astounding, "No! We want to stay and play. Don't make us go!" I told them I would let them stay, but they would have to behave and not show themselves to people any more. They promised me they would behave, but just as I expected, they wouldn't keep their promise.

One week later, the children appeared to Janice, a newly-hired nurse who had recently moved to our city from out of state. I was in the medication room when she entered and exclaimed:

I swear this place is haunted. I was in the hallway on

my way to my patient's room when I saw several little kids run into the room, but when I got there, they were gone. I asked my patient if he had seen the children run into his room and he said, "What children?" I know I saw them.

I told her I believed her because I had seen them too and so had several other people. I informed her that this wing had been the pediatric unit before it became the second wing for the cardiovascular unit.

She said:

Well that explains it. I thought my last hospital was haunted, but this place is really gonna be a doozy. I can see it now. These little ghost children are gonna try and drive me crazy. I'll just have to send them on their way.

I turned around and looked at her while she was still taking meds out of the Pyxis. I told her I was a psychic medium and I perceived she was too. She stopped pulling meds, looked at me and said:

I see that the two of us are gonna be dealing with the ghost kids. They told me you said they can stay if they behave, but the way I see it, they're never gonna behave. So maybe we should just send them on their way.

I took a deep breath and let it out slowly. I thought about how the children seemed perfectly happy here playing with each other and they really didn't wreak too much havoc. I hated the thought of making them go even though I knew it would be better for their soul evolution if they moved on to a higher plane. I actually loved having these ghost children around. I am very maternalistic at heart and I knew I would miss them once they were gone, but I had to do what was right for them. I suggested to Janice that we should approach the children together and lovingly call in angels and loved one to take them to heaven. I told her I felt it was vitally important the children know they can continue to play together in heaven. We agreed to meet in the staff lounge after work and cross the them over.

Immediately after clocking out, I went to the staff lounge and waited for Janice to arrive. Once she showed up, we had to wait another five minutes for the night shift to finish putting their personal belongings away and leave the lounge. Once the coast was clear, we agreed on how we were to proceed in crossing the children over. We joined hands while I said a prayer of protection and called upon God, the angels, and loved ones to come and rescue these sweet little souls who had not crossed over because of their desire to stay and play. We imagined filling the whole wing with white light and called out to the children for them to come to us. We told them that it was time for them to play in heaven and that they would have a lot of fun because there was so much more to play with there. We visualized and showed them a beautiful playground with all kinds of playground equipment such as balls, swings, and monkey bars they could climb. We told them they would never have to be cooped up inside a hospital building ever again, and it was time for them to play outdoors in heaven.

We watched as their angels and loved ones, surrounded by golden light, gathered them together and took them to heaven ascending on fluffy white clouds. We continued to listen to these little ones as they said thank you and goodbye until their sweet voices faded completely away. We both had tears in our eyes as we said goodbye to them, promising that we would see them again one day in heaven. I left the hospital that evening feeling elated because I had a new psychic friend and the ghost children I cared so much about were finally in heaven where they belong.

Shadow Figures Haunt the Critical Care Wing

During my career as a nurse, I worked on a 32 bed critical care unit. This was a fast-paced, vigilant, no-nonsense unit. Our patients were seriously ill, and anyone one of them could die at any moment. Having three patients code at the same time was not unusual. We ran our own codes on the unit and had two code team assignments each shift. Everyday, the code team assignment changed and the nurses were given a different role from the day before. For instance, if a nurse was assigned the role of IV/IO med nurse the previous day, she might be assigned the role of monitor/defibrillator nurse on the current day. We also had two backup hospital code teams made up of emergency department doctors and nurses. Fortunately for us, one of the hospital code teams had always been available to respond immediately to a third simultaneous code when we needed them. On one unbelievable shift we had ten codes. Before then, I think the most we had ever had in one day was five. Three of the ten patients that coded were on ventilators and died from cardiac arrest that couldn't be reversed. A ventilator will keep a person breathing, but it won't keep the heart going if it is irreversibly damaged. Being on a vent has no benefit when there is no circulation of blood to disseminate oxygen to the tissues. Of the seven patients that weren't on ventilators, only three were successfully resuscitated, the other four passed away. A total of seven patients died that shift.

At the end of each shift, the staff, both the nurses and CNAs (Certified Nursing Assistants), converged in the lounge to chat, retrieve personal belongings, clock out, and go home. Most of us were already in the staff lounge when Nurse Ebony walked in, closed the door behind her, and exclaimed:

> What the hell is going on? What happened today? It's those damn shadow people! They're working overtime! Now I know why I've been seeing so many of them flitting around the last few days.

All three of Ebony's patients coded and died that day. She was very attuned to the spirit world, and probably could have hung out her shingle as a medium. Ebony wasn't the only one to witness these shadow people. Several of our critical care staff members had reported seeing at least one during their employment on our unit. For me, I would see at least one shadow figure every shift I worked. They were always there hanging around those patients closest to death. I believe the presence of these shadow figures can be a harbinger of death. Most of the ones I saw on the unit looked humanoid but with different and distinguishable silhouettes; however, a few looked like fuzzy ink blobs with a head and limbs. Some looked like the Quaker Oats man with his broad brimmed hat and cape, others looked like monks with hooded robes, and a few resembled nuns wearing a habit and veil.

Not all shadow figures look scary or foreboding to me; some look like regular everyday people. Sometimes I would see a shadow figure that looked like an angel hovering over a patient's bed. These shadow angels are usually at least seven feet tall with wings that seemed to span six feet across at its widest point. I came to associate this shadow angel as the angel of death. Whenever I saw one of these angels, the patient it hovered over usually died within twenty-four hours. Whenever I saw a humanoid shadow figure, the patient would either make a miraculous recovery or die within a few days.

Most of the staff chose not to hang out in the lounge after work that evening just to listen to, or talk about death and shadow figures, so they went home. Those of us who remained were very eager to share our work encounters with shadow figures. Of course Ebony, being the outspoken and animated person she is, jumped at the chance to go first. This is her story:

I had only been out of nursing school for about a year

when I saw my first shadow figure on the medical-surgical unit at this very hospital. My patient, who had lung cancer, had her left lower lobe removed. She was only about 38 years old and she had never smoked. Anyway, she seemed to be doing well. Her chest tube had been removed three days earlier and the discharge plan in the doctor's progress note indicated that she would be discharged to home in a couple of days if she continued to do well. After report I went by her room and eyeballed her from the door to make sure she was okay. She seemed to be sleeping soundly. Her respirations were even and unlabored on two liters of oxygen via nasal cannula. As I started to walk away, I noticed out of the corner of my eye a dark shadow hovering over her. I turned back around and looked directly at it, and it was still there. I stood there for what seemed like an eternity unable to move out of fear. I shook my head a couple of times thinking that my imagination was playing tricks on me, but it wasn't. The creature was still there. It looked like an angel, but it was solid black. The shadow angel looked up at me briefly and then vanished into thin air right before my eyes.

I took the vital sign sheet from behind the door and noticed that her blood pressure was elevated at 172/94. Her baseline average was 120/80. Her heart rate was 102 when it had averaged in the 80's. Her oral temp was 96.4. My patient's vitals indicated that she might be going into septic shock, a blood infection that can quickly lead to organ failure and death if not treated promptly. I walked over to the side of the bed to get a closer look at her. She was resting with her eyes closed. Her respirations were even and unlabored at 28 respirations per minute. I walked out of the room and down the hall to the nurses' station where her CNA was standing. I asked her to immediately get another set of vitals signs on Mrs. Smith. She did and the results were worse than before. Her blood pressure was now 200/120; her heart rate was 110; her respirations were 36 and her axillary temp was 93.8 degrees Fahrenheit. My patient was definitely going into septic shock.

I called the doctor and received stat orders for labs, blood cultures, and IV antibiotics. I also received an order to transfer her to the ICU once her blood draws were complete and her antibiotics were hung. The doctor complimented us on acting quickly to recognize and treat her sepsis, but unfortunately she still died in the ICU that evening from a pulmonary embolism.

Ever since then, I know that when I see a shadow figure around a patient, it is a death omen. This incident happened ten years ago. After that, I only saw a few of them out of the corner of my eye for the remainder of my time working on that unit. I have worked this unit for the last two years, and I can't remember a shift when I didn't see them directly with my central vision. This wing is infested with them.

With excitement in his voice, Chris spoke up next and eagerly started to tell the story of his first encounter with shadow figures at work. Chris was one of the best CNAs we had on our unit. Whenever he was assigned to my patients, I knew they would receive the best care possible from him. This is his story:

When I first became a CNA, I worked the evening shift at a very nice private nursing home that catered to the rich. All the rooms were single occupancy, large, and very luxurious. I was frequently assigned to a resident named Mrs. Stuart. She was receiving hospice care because she had bone cancer that had metastasized from her lungs and was now all over her body.

Early one evening when I helped her to bed, she told me she had seen her mother and aunt in the room that afternoon. I thought maybe she might be hallucinating from some of the strong pain medication she was receiving as part of her hospice regimen, so I just indulged her and asked her where in her room she saw them.

She said, "Oh, they were standing over there." She pointed to the far corner of the room.

I asked her if she had any other visitors.

She said, "My paternal grandma came to see me last night. She said she would be coming to get me soon and take me home."

I then asked her if her if her grandma was still alive.

She looked at me with a puzzled expression and said, "Of course she isn't. She died sixty years ago."

That made a lot of sense to me because my patient was 87 years old.

What I experienced when I opened the door to check on her during my 10 p.m. rounds that night would forever change my beliefs about spirits and the afterlife. I saw a weird shadow sliding across the wall. I've never seen a shadow move the way this one did. It seemed to have consciously moved away from the light coming in from the hallway when I opened the door. It settled in the far corner of the room near the ceiling and hung upside down like a bat. It had wings and red eyes that glowed like embers of burning wood. It filled me with a sense of intense dread and fear.

I then looked over at Mrs. Stuart and saw a group of about seven shadow figures bending over her bed. Unlike the wall shadow, these shadows looked like people. I could make out the silhouette of most of them. Five looked like women in dresses with short, fluffy hairdos, and a two looked like men in suits with wide brim hats. Although these shadow people looked spooky, I wasn't afraid of them. I thought that maybe they were just dead relatives that had come to help Mrs. Stuart die and cross over. I don't know what the bat looking creature was all about. Anyway, she died the next morning. The day shift CNA told me when I came to work that afternoon that she died peacefully. I hope her spirit is at rest and she's not somehow being tormented by the bat shadow.

That was five years ago, and I haven't seen anymore shadow figures with wings that hang upside down. However, I have seen a lot of shadow people since I started work here three years ago. It's not unusual for me see at least one each week, but I have probably seen close to ten in the last few days. I have to agree with Ebony—this wing is infested with shadow figures.

Marilyn was the next to tell her story. She had worked as an inpatient hospice nurse for five years at another facility before coming to work on the medical-surgical unit of our hospital for two years. Then she went to work on the cardiac step-down for one year before transferring to our unit to train as a critical care nurse. This is her story:

I had been a nurse for about six months when I saw my first shadow figure, and I have been seeing them ever since. A month after I passed my RN boards, I got a job working the night shift at a 160 bed hospice facility. I was assigned seven patients on the night of my first encounter with a shadow figure. All of my patients had less than six months to live, but one of them, Mrs. Walters, was already at death's door. She was sixty-seven years old and dying from brain cancer. She slipped into a coma within several minutes after her last seizure twelve hours earlier. She was still in a coma when I started my shift.

When I performed her p.m. assessment that evening, her respirations were shallow but even and unlabored on two liters of oxygen per nasal cannula. She was extremely pale and slightly cyanotic (blue) around her lips. She had some skin mottling on her lower extremities, but none on her abdomen or arms. It had been over twelve house since the last time she urinated. I knew from my assessment that she was actively dying; I just didn't know how much time she had left. I took her hand and lightly squeezed it. I told her my name and that I would be with her all night. I also told her that I would be praying for her. The day shift nurse told me she called the daughter who lived several states away to let her know her mother had made a turn for the worse. The daughter said it would probably take her a couple of days to get here, but she would do her best to arrive sooner if possible. Her daughter was her only living relative. Sadly, there was no one else.

I was sitting at the desk in my foyer when I heard screams and crying coming from Mrs. Walter's room. I ran over to the entrance of her door and looked into her dimly lit room. She was sitting straight up in her bed. Her eyes were wide open and she was screaming, "No! No! No! Don't let them take me! Go away! Go Away!" My eyes were then drawn to the huge black mass swirling a couple of feet above her head. I couldn't believe my eyes. I looked away and then back again. It was still there. I wanted to run over and comfort her, but my feet felt like they were stuck in cement. I couldn't move, but I could speak. I commanded it to move away from her in the name of Jesus. I commanded twice more before I got a reaction from it. It became much bigger and charged directly at me. There must have been a hundred devilish looking faces within this mass and they all had glowing red eyes. I have never been so scared in all my life. I trembled all over, but I didn't back down. I continued to command this thing to go back to hell and leave my patient alone in the name of Jesus. I told the devils in this black shadow that they couldn't have my patient because I was intervening for her soul and calling on the holy angels to take her to God where she would be saved by His grace. Once again, I heard screams but they weren't coming from my patient. They were coming from the demons inside the shadow figure. They continued to scream, shriek, and hiss for a few seconds before they vanished from my sight. My patient collapsed back onto her bed.

I called upon Archangel Michael to come and protect my patient's soul and take her to heaven so that she could have one last chance at being saved. I saw a flash of light just above her head. The room became much lighter and the fragrance of roses permeated the air.

I knew then that Archangel Michael had rescued my patient's soul from eternal torment. I walked over and took her hand in mine, and as I did she took her last breath with a smile on her face. I hung my head and thanked God for bestowing grace on my patient. I knew by the smile on her face that she was in paradise. The fragrance of roses continued to linger in that room until the funeral home attendants picked up her body.

You could have heard a pin drop in that staff lounge. We were all totally amazed by Marilyn's encounter with the demon shadow and her spiritual prowess in banishing it. I was the last to tell the story of my first encounter with a shadow figure while at work. This is what happened:

I have seen shadow figures darting about out of the corner of my eyes for as long as I can remember. But, my first encounter with a shadow figure at work occurred while I was employed as a registered nurse on the cardiac step-down unit of a large medical center. I had been assigned four post-op open heart surgical patients. All of them were stable and on target for the third post-op day Coronary Arterial Bypass Graft (CABG) clinical pathway. I felt my patients were doing well enough for me to get lunch in the cafeteria, so I had the nurse in the next foyer to listen out for them until I came back.

As soon as I returned to the floor, I got a quick report on the status of my patients from the nurse covering for me. She said that she had eyeballed them and they seemed to be okay, and no one called for anything. When I got back to my foyer, I checked on all four patients. They all had visitors and appeared to be well.

Mr. Thomas was the last patient I checked on. When I walked into his room, he and his wife were smiling and holding hands. She was sitting in a chair on the left side of his bed; on the right side of his bed was a shadow figure that appeared to be kneeling down on the floor. The silhouette of this shadow figure was solid gray and looked like a nun wearing a habit and veil. It was spooky, but I didn't get a feeling of evil from it. Mrs. Thomas asked me how her husband was doing and told me that she had asked the parishioners and nuns at church to say prayers for her husband. I told her that her husband was doing well, and I believed the prayers of the nuns were being heard.

Later that shift around 6 p.m. after his wife left the hospital to go home, Mr. Thomas went into ventricular fibrillation (V-fib). This lethal rhythm will quickly lead to death if not converted in a timely manner. V-fib is an abnormal heart rhythm in which the ventricles (bottom chambers of the heart) quiver instead of pumping normally. Fifteen seconds before the telemetry tech called to let me know about the potentially fatal rhythm, I looked up at the monitors above my desk and watched as Mr. Thomas' normal sinus rhythm morphed into the deadly rhythm. I immediately called a code, and by the time I got to his room with the crash cart from my foyer, it was full of shadow nuns, kneeling and standing by his bed. They all had rosary beads in their hands.

I initiated chest compressions per the most current CPR protocol of that time, and within a few more seconds the whole code team arrived and we initiated the ACLS (Advanced Cardiac Life Support) algorithm. After administering the first shock, he returned to a sustained normal sinus rhythm in the 80's. We drew labs and sent Mr. Thomas to the Coronary Care Unit (CCU) for closer observation. The shadow nuns definitely intervened through prayer for Mr. Thomas that day. A few days later, he was discharged home from the CCU.

No one really knows for sure what shadow figures are. Some paranormal investigators postulate that they could be earthbound ghosts, guides, spirits of the living who have projected into the astral realm, or extra-terrestrial beings. Shadow people are probably the most reported type of shadow figure. Just as there are reports of good and evil ghosts, we can also assume there are good and evil shadow figures. Many people who have reported witnessing a shadow figure say they got bad vibes and believed it was an evil spirit or demon. Others who have seen one say they got good vibes and had a good experience. Shadow figures may be seen as an unrecognizable fleeting mist, a blob, an orb, an angel, or as a humanoid figure. Not all shadow figures are black. I have seen white, blue, and gray shadows as well as black ones. They also have varying degrees of solidity. Some are more translucent than others. Most of the time, they are seen peripherally out of the corner of the eyes, but can sometimes be seen straight ahead with the direct gaze of the eyes. One point everyone who has seen a shadow figure agrees upon is they can be downright scary. This response is only natural since the sighting of something creepy and unknown instinctively arouses fear in the human mind—we fear what we do not understand.

~ Three ~

GHOST DOCTORS STILL AT WORK

"Our feet are planted in the real world, but we dance with angels and ghosts."
— John Cameron Mitchell

The Disgruntled Surgeon

Many hospitals experience phases of building or remodeling. This was the case at a large urban hospital where I worked. The current hospital looks nothing like the original, which was built in 1960. On this particular day, I had been floated from the orthopedic unit on the sixth floor of the main hospital to the adjoining acute care rehab hospital. Ten years earlier, the second floor of the rehab hospital housed the pre-op, post-op, and surgical suites. I wasn't happy to hear that I was being sent to 2C at the rehab hospital. This unit specialized in fresh traumatic neurological injuries in stabilized patients, and required much physical activity as most of the patient population was either paraplegic or quadriplegic. I knew it was going to be a physically and emotionally draining day. It's hard to witness the sorrows of this patient population. No matter what type of day I thought I was going to have, it would be pure joy compared to what many of my patients experienced on a daily basis, which was pure hell.

While receiving report from the off-going night nurse, I heard the voice of a disgruntled dead doctor screaming in my ear, "Damn it! That patient shouldn't have died on the table! It's the nurse's fault! Why didn't she let us know that he had been complaining of headaches and blurred vision! Someone must be held accountable for this atrocity!" I allowed this doctor to rant for a little while longer before I audibly told him to, "Shut up. I have my own patients to take care of!"

Of course, the night nurse giving me report was not happy with my comment. Her face turned blood red, she jumped up, pulled her chair against the wall, and said, "If you have a problem with what I'm saying, we need to take it to the charge nurse."

I realized what I had done and immediately apologized to her. I tried to explain to her without totally humiliating myself that I was talking to a ghost and not her.

She looked down her nose at me and said, "Look, I don't know what your problem is, I just want to give you report and go home."

I told her my only problem was I sometimes had ghosts come to me with their concerns. I explained to her I was sensitive to the spirit world, and I was telling the ghost of a disgruntled surgeon to shut up, not her.

She glared at me with a quizzical look on her face and said, "I guess it takes all kinds!"

I told her I couldn't understand why a surgeon would be coming to me in a rehab hospital.

She said, "You know, before it was a rehab hospital, the whole second floor was once pre-op, post-op and operating suites for the main hospital."

The night nurse glared at me once more for a few seconds, stood up, and said, "I have to go home. I don't have time for such nonsense!" I was never asked to float to the rehab hospital again.

The Ghost of Dr. Smith Barks Orders That Kill!

While I was a nurse on the mother/baby unit of a county hospital I'll refer to as Jay Memorial, I worked with a new nurse named Vicky who had been out of school for only four months. She was assigned a preeclamptic patient who was seven months pregnant. Preeclampsia is a pregnancy complication characterized by high blood pressure and signs of damage to other organ systems, most often the liver and kidneys. Preeclampsia usually begins after twenty weeks of pregnancy in women whose blood pressure had been normal. Left untreated, preeclampsia can lead to serious, even fatal, complications for both mother and baby. Preeclampsia often leads to eclampsia, which is defined as the occurrence of generalized seizures in a woman with preexisting preeclampsia.

Two days after her hospitalization, this patient became

eclamptic and started having severe uncontrollable seizures. She had been receiving IV magnesium sulfate, the treatment of choice, to control her seizures for more than a week and had unknowingly become toxic by the time Vicky had her as a patient. Either a magnesium level had not been drawn on this patient, or an elevated magnesium level went unchecked.

Vicky made a deadly mistake that would haunt her forever when she acted on a verbal order given by the ghost of Dr. Smith. This is the story she told me in the staff lounge before she was relieved of duty that day:

> During my morning assessment of Mrs. Stanley, she complained of nausea, blurred vision and extreme weakness. I also noticed she had some trouble forming her words. At the time, I didn't realize that these were all symptoms of magnesium toxicity. Anyway, I quickly went in search of the doctor I had just seen walk by the patient's door. I caught up with him the the hallway and told him about my patient's symptoms. He barked orders at me to give a one time dose of magnesium 2 mg. IV in addition to the patient's routine magnesium order, and then he walked away. I gave the drug per the doctor's verbal order, not realizing he was a ghost.
>
> The patient went into cardiac arrest not long after the drug was given. A code was called—we were able to resuscitate the patient and reverse her apparent magnesium toxicity by giving her 1 gram of calcium gluconate. Fortunately for me and everyone involved, the patient and her unborn baby survived this ordeal (the patient gave birth to a healthy baby girl one month later). Of course, the supervisor, Mrs. Aycock, wrote

me up for administering drugs without a doctor's order and put me on probation. I maintained that I did have an order—a verbal order—and that the old doctor who was making rounds on the floor ordered me to give the magnesium. I gave Mrs. Aycock a description of the doctor, and my description eerily matched that of a mother/baby doctor she knew who had died three years earlier. Mrs. Aycock asked me if this doctor had JAS embroidered on his lab coat. I thought about it for a minute and exclaimed with excitement, "Yes, he did! He most certainly did! Now you know I'm telling the truth! He gave me a verbal order!"

Mrs. Aycock said to me, "Honey, he couldn't have given you the order—his name was Dr. James Allen Smith, and he died three years ago. He was a very competent and respected doctor. You're not the first nurse to encounter the ghost of Dr. Smith and you won't be the last, but please be sure of the name of the doctor and credentials and right to practice in our hospital before you take anymore verbal orders. Also be sure to only take verbal orders from a doctor during an emergency and have that doctor write the order before they leave the hospital. I know we haven't written anything in our policy yet about when it's appropriate to take a verbal order, but we are working on it as a patient safety initiative. In the meantime, just don't take any verbal order unless it is a valid emergency and the charge nurse and doctor are present with the patient. It's just good practice. Never act alone in an emergency. There is strength and safety in numbers. Use your charge nurse; that's why she's there!"

Vicky was relieved from duty for the rest of the shift. I sat with her a few minutes in the staff lounge while she cried on my shoulder before going home. I told her every-thing was going to be okay because she was a very smart nurse, nursing was hard, and she should hang in there. I also told her I had seen Dr. Smith roaming down the hall on the mother/baby unit and so had several other sensi-tive nurses. I told her I wished someone had warned her about the ghost of Dr. Smith so she could have been pre-pared for the encounter.

Vicky's reply was, "Mrs. Aycock said he was a very competent and respected doctor. If that's the case, why did he give me such bad orders?"

I told Vicky Dr. Smith had to stop practicing medicine a couple of years before he died because he was diagnosed with Alzheimers.

With tears welling up in her eyes again, she said, "Well, I guess that explains why he gave me such a bad order. I swear he seemed so real!"

I told Vicky that I had the gift of mediumship and she apparently had the gift too. I also told her that I would help her anyway I could to understand and use her gift. Several of our sensitive nurses continued to see Dr. Smith on the unit, but no one took orders from the ghost doctor who refused to give up his practice.

Dr. Adams—The Poltergeist!

I made daily rounds on my patients with Dr. Adams—a well respected heart surgeon—in the cardiac care step-down unit of the large medical center where I worked. Dr. Adams had a wonderful reputation for being the best open heart surgeon in the area; he also had a reputation among the nurses for being ill tempered and throwing things. All the nurses dreaded seeing him come on the unit each day because they knew he would create some kind of drama. For example, I was standing at my desk early one afternoon planning care with my CNA when Dr. Adams approached me and started screaming about why we never stocked bottles of alcohol on the unit anymore:

I am damn tired of the way things are being managed around here! Why can't y'all stock bottles of alcohol anymore? Your nurse buddy in the next foyer refused to get me a bottle of alcohol and then tried to get me to use prep pads. I don't need prep pads! I need a whole damn bottle of alcohol! Why is that so difficult?"

He had a chart in his hand he had taken from last patient foyer he visited and threw it down on my desk. "Here, how 'bout putting that back on the rack for me and get me some damn alcohol!" I knew we didn't have any in our stock room, so I called the cardiology unit, which was across the main hall from my unit and asked the secretary if they had a bottle I could get for Dr. Adams. She said they did and I could come pick it up at their main desk. I asked the nurse in the foyer next to me to listen out for my patients while I went to retrieve the alcohol. As soon as I got back, I paged Dr. Adams to pick up his alcohol. When he arrived fifteen minutes later, I gave him the bottle, which he took and threw down the hall. He said, "I needed that damn alcohol an hour ago! I don't need it now!" The bottle hit the wall and burst open, splattering the contents on the wall and floor. Dr. Adams continued walking down the hall and stepped over the puddle of alcohol as if it was no big deal.

I filled out an incident report describing his aggressive behavior and informed my charge nurse. I didn't really expect that there would be any type of reprimand because other nurses had filled out incident reports too and nothing ever changed. Apparently, our risk management department didn't see his behavior as being violent and a possible physical threat to the staff. His actions could have definitely caused physical harm had someone been hit in the head with the bottle, especially if the alcohol splattered in their eyes. In addition to being physically abusive, he was definitely psychologically and verbally abusive. His rants and throwing behaviors continued worse than ever after the alcohol incident until he died six months later in a plane crash. He was returning home from a month long vacation in Europe with his wife who was thirty years his junior.

One month after Dr. Adams died in the plane crash, we started experiencing poltergeist activity on the unit. At first, the activity seemed to center around Sarah—our unit secretary. One day during lunch in the staff lounge, she told me and several other nurses about several recent incidents of charts flying out of her chart rack and landing on the floor; the cabinet doors of her desk would fly open with a multitude of forms spewing out everywhere; and her coffee would tip over for no reason. She said when these events occurred, she felt the same way she felt when Dr. Adams was close by—uptight and very nervous. One of the nurses having lunch with us who always loved giving Sarah a hard time said, "Oh Sarah, are you sure you're not just clumsy?" Another nurse who thought she was being funny said, "I bet you're being haunted by the ghost of one of the patients you killed when you were a CNA."

I looked up at Sarah and told her she was having the same feelings she had when Dr. Adams was around because her intuition was telling her the ghost of Dr. Adams was causing the activity. Everyone in that staff lounge became deathly quiet—you could have heard a pin drop—until James came bursting through the door. James had worked with us several years as a CNA before recently finishing nursing school and becoming a RN on our unit. He popped his lunch in the microwave and sat down at the long, wide table with the rest of us.

He looked around and said, "Wow! Y'all look like ya'll just seen a ghost!"

Sarah looked over at James and said, "Wow James! You must be psychic! How could you possibly know?"

With his head cocked to one side, James gave Sarah a quizzical look and said in his strong southern accent, "What cha talking bout girl? You seen a ghost?"

James listened attentively as Sarah told him about the poltergeist activity she was experiencing at her desk. The microwave alarm sounded just as Sarah was finishing her story. James jumped up, got his lunch out and sat back down without saying a word. He opened his Tupperware lunch plate, took a bite of his ribs, potato salad, and collard greens and then said:

Girl, are ya serious! That's so damn freaky! I was talking a to scrub nurse, circulating nurse, and surgical tech in the cafeteria the other day who all worked on Dr. Adams's team—they only scrubbed in on Dr. Adams' cases. They were talking bout how things are getting pretty damn crazy in O.R. #2 since he died. That was the only O.R. he worked out of because it was set up just the way he wanted it. Dr. Anderson has taken over Dr. Adams patients and does surgery in O.R. #2 now. Apparently, Dr. Adams doesn't like the way Dr. Anderson performs surgery. The scrub nurse said she firmly placed a scalpel in Dr. Anderson's hand and it went flying across the room. The two of them looked at each other like, "What the hell?" She gave him another scalpel and the same thing happened. Then she told Dr. Adams out loud she was sorry he didn't like the way they did surgery, but he was dead and had to leave them alone because he was putting the patient's life at risk. After she spoke her mind to Dr. Adams, the third scalpel she firmly placed in Dr. Anderson's hand stayed and the room became much warmer. The O.R. can get really cold sometime, but she said it was a lot colder than usual when all this activity was happening—to the point where they were all shivering.

That's not the only thing that's happened down there—the circulating nurse said she pulled three sterile packages containing surgical instruments out of the storage closet and placed them on the counter for the scrub nurse to set up her field. When she turned her back to walk away, all three of the packages flew off the counter and hit the floor five feet away. Bewildered, she went to the closet and pulled out more packages of instruments. About that time, the scrub nurse walked in and the circulating nurse told her that if she wanted sterile instruments, she had better go ahead and set up her field before Dr. Adams threw another temper tantrum. The scrub nurse looked at her and said with her Jamaican accent, "Oh no, you don't mean that crazy ghost doctor is at it again. I am definitely gonna exorcise his ass!"

The surgical tech said he was putting packs of instruments in the autoclave and when he turned around to get more from the tray behind him, the ones he had already put in there came flying out, one at a time. He said he had to jump out of the way to keep from getting hit. There wasn't a single pack of instruments left in there, not one—they were all on the floor on the other side of the O.R., near the double doors.

I was taking out a chest tube, and had a sterile drape set up on the over-bed table with everything I needed on it—a suture removal kit, gauze, xeroform impregnated gauze, regular gauze and tape. Betty, the charge nurse was with me because I haven't taken out many chest tubes. I put on my sterile gloves, picked up the suture removal scissors and tweezer and bent over my patient. I had just removed the sutures when my whole sterile drape went flying off the table. I thought that maybe I had somehow inadvertently knocked it off, but Betty said I was no where near the table. The whole drape and everything on it just flew off. That happened about a month after Dr. Adams died, before I heard about anyone else's story. It had to be him. He is even more of an asshole in death than he was in life!

Fortunately for me, I didn't experience any of Dr. Adams's ghostly temper tantrums or poltergeist activity. Maybe he left me alone because I had always tried to assist him anyway I could for the good of our patients. Also, I kept my cool and never challenged him. He never gave me an order that would have resulted in harm to my patients. I don't know why Dr. Adams is wreaking havoc in the O.R. Maybe he doesn't like Dr. Anderson or his surgical technique, but I do know why he might be haunting the unit secretary. I have overheard her speak to Dr. Adams with a harsh tone of voice on several occasions. She would make comments such as: "I don't have time for that crap! Why don't you ask one of the lazy nurses to help you?" I have also overheard several nurses make ugly comments to Dr. Adams such as: "This is not the 1950's—I'm not your personal errand girl" and "I have patients to take care of; I don't have time for your mess." The comments they made were very unprofessional and did not help the situation much. All he really wanted was someone to help him get what he needed to provide care to our patients. I believe mutual respect is vital to fostering good work relationships, or any relationship for that matter. Dr. Adams didn't show respect to the staff members on our unit, but sometimes appeasing a narcissist is easier than getting caught up in their drama. Since Dr. Adams left me alone, I decided it was in my best interest was to leave him alone to spend eternity in hospital purgatory. Needless to say, I didn't try to cross him over.

~ Four ~

GHOSTS OF DEDICATED NURSES

"The popular notion that ghosts are likely to be seen in a graveyard is not borne out by psychical research.... A haunting ghost usually haunts a place that a person lived in or frequented while alive.... Only a gravedigger's ghost would be likely to haunt a graveyard."

—John Alexander, *Ghosts! Washington Revisited: The Ghostlore of the Nation's Capitol*

Nurse Abigail is Still Caring for Spanish Flu Patients

I first encountered Nurse Abigail on the back hall of the medical-surgical unit at about three o'clock in the morning. I had volunteered to work as a staff nurse on the floor while we were in the process of closing down the hospital. Many staff nurses had resigned upon the news release that we were not going to be able to to build a new hospital because we were denied the Certificate of Need from the state to do so. We would be unable to keep our doors open for very much longer because the building that housed our hospital was considered to be functionally obsolete and unsafe. According to certain regulatory authorities, our hallways were too narrow to handle an emergency evacuation situation, and to top that off, we didn't even have a sprinkler system. To continue as a hospital, we needed a new facility. We had the financing for a new hospital, but we didn't have the Certificate of Need.

As I stated earlier, it was three o'clock in the morning, and I had just purchased a can of Diet Mountain Dew out of the vending machine in the surgical waiting room. When I walked out of the waiting room and back into the hall, I saw the ghost of Nurse Abigail stick her head out of an empty patient room. I blinked my eyes several times and wondered if I might be sleepwalking. I told myself to wake up, but I still saw her as she walked out of that room and proceeded slowly down the hall peeking into each room as she went. I took a sip of my Mountain Dew and concluded that I was very much awake. When I passed Abigail, she noticed me, quickly turned around and came towards me. I thought to myself, oh no, she sees me. As Abigail came closer, I noticed that she was wearing a light blue, long-sleeved cotton dress that hung down to her ankles. A white pinafore apron covered her dress. On her feet, she wore black lace-up shoes with a 2-inch heel. Wrapped around her head was a white cotton scarf tied at the nape of her neck.

Looking straight at me she said: "You can see me, can't you?"

I replied, "Yes I can."

I asked her what her name was, and she said, "My name is Abigail and I am a nurse here at this Hospital."

I said, "Okay. What year is it?"

She replied, "It's 1918, and you sure are dressed funny. What and who are you? Are you from the future? Don't tell anybody but sometimes I see things in the future. Are you one of my visions?"

I replied, "I am also a nurse and the current year is 2003. It sounds like you have a gift from God known as precognition, which means you are able to perceive future events. I have abilities from God too, but mine includes being able to see spirits."

I asked her if she remembered passing away? She said, "No, I don't remember dying. I know that I was very sick while I continued to care for my patients with the influenza. I haven't seen any angels or anybody that I know. I think I may have died from the grippe (Spanish Influenza Epidemic of 1918), but if I died, shouldn't I be in heaven?"

I said, "That's what normally happens, but sometimes we get so caught up in our work we become attached to it and can't let go of the earth plane. If you want me to, I could call for the angels to come and take you to heaven."

She replied, "What if I'm not good enough to go to heaven?"

I told her, "God is gracious and anyone who wants to go to heaven can. God does not judge us—we judge ourselves. God loves and accepts everyone who desires grace."

She said, "Okay, I guess I can trust you."

In my mind, I called out to the Holy Angels and loved

ones in Spirit to take her sweet soul to God in Heaven. I asked them to let her feel God's love and acceptance before they crossed her over so she would know without any doubts she was on her way to heaven, not hell. No sooner had I mentally uttered this prayer, than she was surrounded by a bluish white light and several beautiful angels dressed in silver robes with gold sashes who escorted her up a winding, pearlescent staircase. She glanced back at me and I heard her say, "Thank you." I told her she was very welcome, and it was my pleasure to help a fellow nurse in need.

Helen, The Award Winning Nurse

I was sitting at the medical-surgical nurses' station performing chart audits when nurse Helen first appeared to me. She had dark blonde hair, blue-green eyes, thin lips, a narrow bridged nose, and an oval-shaped face. Nurse Helen was not working that day. She had not worked for several decades because she was dead. Helen was on a mission to get a message to her husband who would be visiting a friend at the hospital later that day. After making her presence known, she said to me in a stern voice, "Pay attention to me and please write down my message. He will be here this afternoon and you must give him the note." So I took out a blank nurses' progress note from the desk drawer in front of me and began to write as she dictated the following message:

Tell him I am so grateful he was my husband in life. I want to thank him for taking such good care of me while I was sick. I know he still loves me and I love him but he's been alone for too long. Tell him it's okay to marry the new lady he's been dating. She will make him very happy. I am moving on to a higher place now. I will no longer be with him in spirit. I release him for all eternity as my husband. I want a divorce. Tell him to let go of me so I can move on.

It was about 10:30 a.m. when Helen made her appearance to me and I recorded her message. When 1:00 p.m. arrived, I joined several of my administrative cohorts at a nearby popular Mexican restaurant where we frequently met for lunch. We had the usual fare, whatever the daily special was, and the usual conversations about family, vacations, special events, and work issues. The waitresses who worked at this restaurant took very good care of us as a group. They always took our orders promptly and served our food quickly, because they knew we needed to get back to work on time. I didn't participate in the conversation as much as I normally did because my thoughts kept returning to Nurse Helen and the message she wanted me to give to her husband.

On the drive back to the hospital, I thought about returning to my office to work on crunching some numbers and doing some statistical analysis for the upcoming Clinical Quality Control meeting scheduled later that week. As soon as I thought of returning to my office, however, Nurse Helen quickly and adamantly chimed in my ear:

You have to go back to the nurses' station. You have to work there so that you can give my husband the message I gave you. He will be there soon. You can get back to your office after that if you want to!

I pulled into my usual assigned parking space close to the cottage-style building that housed several administrative offices, including my own. I hearkened to the voice of Helen and walked back over to the main hospital, which was on the other side of the small parking lot. The med/surg unit seemed to be unusually calm as I walked down the hallway towards the nurses' station. The secretary was sitting in her usual chair at the front counter when I arrived. There were plenty of places for me to sit and audit charts. Helen chimed in once again and told me that I needed to sit behind the secretary close to the counter facing the hallway. After I had audited several charts, I glanced up at the clock and noted it was already 4 p.m. I thought to myself, *if he doesn't come within the next 15 minutes I'm going back to my office.* No sooner than I had that thought, Helen broke through and said "Just wait, he's on the way now. He should be here in about five minutes." I sat there and periodically glanced up at the clock.

Sure enough, five minutes later Helen's husband came strolling up to the nurse's station and introduced himself to the secretary. He said he wanted to stop by for old times sake. He began talking about his dead wife who had passed away two decades earlier. They both worked at the hospital before she became ill. He worked days as a maintenance man and she worked evenings as a medical surgical nurse. He would stop by the nurse's station everyday and have dinner with her when he got off from work before going home. Of course, my ears perked up, and I listened as he continued to talk to the secretary about his deceased wife. He said she won an award one year for being the most dedicated nurse at the hospital. Every year, the hospital would give an award in recognition of their most dedicated nurse. He said, "See that plaque hanging on the wall right there." He pointed to the back wall in the doctor's charting room behind me. "That was her award." I turned around to look and sure enough, a wooden plaque hanging on the wall had Helen Jones's name on it. I had never taken notice of it before.

At that point, I stood up, walked over to the counter and introduced myself. I told him I needed to speak with him briefly and indicated we should move down the hallway, away from the nurse's station. We walked to the end of the hallway and stood over to one side. I pulled the note out of my lab jacket, unfolded it, and handed it to him. I told him I depended on my job for income and that giving messages on the job was rare. I asked him to please keep this interaction between us a secret because no one at work knew about this aspect of me.

He cocked his head to the side and looked at me with an expression of bewilderment. He didn't say anything to me but started reading the note. A few moments later, he looked up at me with a tear stained face and exclaimed,

Oh my God! There's this lady that I have been seeing for

the last few years and I want to marry her, but I felt as if I would be betraying my dead wife if I did. Thank you for giving me this message. I know it's really okay to move on now. Don't worry, I won't tell anybody about our conversation, but please don't avoid your gift.

After my conversation with Mr. Jones, I walked back towards the nurses' station wondering how I was supposed to use this gift. At that time, there were no t.v. mediums, and it never occurred to me that some people make a career out of giving these kind of messages professionally. They're called mediums.

Nurse Wilkins is Still Making Hospital Rounds!

I encountered the ghost of the former hospital house supervisor, Ms. Wilkins, several times while I was working at Jay County Hospital. I rotated days and nights on the orthopedic and mother/baby units. Of course, I never saw her on the day shift. Only on the night shift around two o'clock in the morning did I see her walking down either the orthopedic hall or the mother/baby hall. I wasn't the only one to witness Ms. Wilkins's apparition. For over forty years, many a sleepy-eyed nurse has seen her apparition roaming the corridors—apparently doing her rounds. Ms. Wilkins always appeared wearing her starchy white dress uniform, white stockings, laced-up white shoes with two inch heels, and winged-style nurse's cap with two black stripes. The rumor was that she was never married, choosing to dedicate her whole life to nursing. As a young nurse, she quickly moved up the ladder from bedside nurse to charge nurse and then hospital supervisor.

Ms. Wilkins usually appeared to me once or twice a week; however, one night I saw her ghost three times in three different places—the mother/baby hall, the orthopedic hall, and the supply room. That same night, when Mrs. Channeler, the current house supervisor, came to the nurse's station to check on us, I asked her if she had seen Mrs. Wilkins's ghost recently. She said:

No, but I wish she was the supervisor tonight instead of me. With exception of you guys, this place has been a mad house! I know there's a full moon, but it has been absolutely ridiculous. There has been one crisis after another starting with the E.R. being slammed and not having enough help. I pulled several nurses from other units and it's still not enough. Now we are on diversion. Then, two ventilators in the ICU started malfunctioning with alarms going off inappropriately and there are no backup ventilators on hand to replace them. I called another hospital, they're going to give us some loaners. Come Monday morning, I'm going to be demanding answers as to why we have no backup ventilators.

The Nephrology unit has ten patients on peritoneal dialysis with not enough of the correct dialysate solution to do individually prescribed dialysis. The nurses had to call and get orders from angry doctors at midnight to administer what they had on hand, which is not the optimal solution for most of their individual patients, and the list goes on. I miss Ms. Wilkins; she was a wonderful house supervisor. She was the one who trained me before she retired. She didn't want to retire, but hospital administration made her. Ms. Wilkins was definitely old school—she never stopped wearing her starchy white dress uniform and cap. I have seen her ghost many times as I make my rounds; it's as if she is rounding with me. She seems to enter my head when I need help the most, especially tonight when I said to myself, *I don't know what to do*. Then, I would sense her presence and know exactly what to do.

I told Mrs. Channeler I figured something was going on in the hospital because I saw Ms. Wilkins's ghost three times tonight. Her reply to me was: "Wow! You're like the third person who has told me they saw her ghost tonight. Apparently, she is still making rounds!" Mrs. Channeler came around to check on us again two hours later and reported that everything seemed to have calmed down, but that heads would definitely roll come Monday morning at the daily administration meeting. Mrs. Channeler never said who the other nurses were who saw Ms. Wilkins that night, but it was comforting to know she was still making rounds. Hospital administration may have made her retire while she was in her physical body, but they couldn't make her retire in her spirit body!

~ Five ~

GHOSTS THAT GET PHYSICAL

"Why do they say ghosts are cold? Mine are warm, a breath dampening your cheek, a voice when you thought you were alone."

— Julie Buntin, *Marlena*

An Icy Cold Chill Down the Left Side of my Body!

Understandably, I have always tried to avoid giving messages while on duty at my nursing job. Not all spirits, however, have shared my agenda. Some spirits persisted until they got their message through to the intended party. On this particular day, I was working on the orthopedic unit and was assigned a patient that had an ORIF (Open Reduction and Internal Fixation) of the right femur a few days earlier and was sitting up in her wheelchair for the first time since her surgery. She was still in a considerable amount of pain, so I was there to give her pain medication. I was standing by her right side when I perceived an intense icy cold chill up and down the left side of my body. I searched around for any air conditioning vents that could have blown a blast of icy cold air on me but there were none. The cold lingered and affected my left side only. The right side of my body felt warm and normal. It was then that I realized an earthbound entity was invading my space.

I telepathically said to this entity, "I know you are there. Who are you?"

He quickly replied, "I am the husband."

I said, "Okay. What do you want?"

He said, "I need to give her a message."

I asked him, "Don't you see my closed sign? I am at work and I can't give your message."

He responded, "Please, you have too. It's a matter of life and death! I will not leave you alone until you give her my message!"

I told him again, "I can't give your message. It might jeopardize my job! I need my job!"

That's when he said to me, "We won't let anything happen to your job."

I quickly responded, "What is this 'we' business?"

He said, "We are the people on this side who love her and are concerned for her well being. She will die before her time if you don't give her the message."

I relented and agreed to give her the message trusting that nothing would happen to my job. I asked this spirit to give me validation of his identity as her husband.

He said, "Tell her that I called her 'Baby' and she called me 'Daddy'."

I prefaced the message to my patient by telling her, "I have a man in spirit with me who says he's your husband and that he called you 'Baby' and you called him 'Daddy'."

He's also telling me he died from a chronic illness that caused him to waste away. I asked her if she wanted to hear the message.

She burst into tears and said, "Yes, of course I do. I lost my husband about six months ago and I miss him so much. He called me 'Baby' and I called him 'Daddy.' He died from AIDS on the fourth floor of this hospital. How could you know?"

I told her, "I know because I have abilities and your husband is standing beside me."

While pointing to her tee shirt, she said, "See this tee shirt. It's a picture of my dead husband. I haven't worn this tee shirt in several months. Why would I be compelled to have my friend bring it to the hospital so I could wear it today?"

I told her, "Maybe it's your husband's way of letting you know that he is with you."

I had not noticed the tee shirt up this point because I was standing beside her. She was also wearing a patient gown over her tee shirt and fleece shorts, which partially covered her tee shirt. The message from her husband continued as follows:

You need to stop hanging out with the crowd you've

been seeing because they are leading you down a destructive path of drugs and alcohol. If you don't, something bad will happen to you very soon. Go back to New York and live with your mother. I know that I wasn't always on the right path and I didn't always go to church, but I'm glad we started going before I died. Please attend church with your mother and make new friends there. I love you and will be with you. I want you to have a full life and find true love again.

At this point my patient was sobbing. With tears streaming down her face, she said:

Everything he's saying is true. My mom has been telling me that I need to go home to New York and start going to church with her because the people I'm hanging with are into drugs. I know something bad is going to happen to me if I don't get away from them and get some help. It's just so hard, and I miss my husband so much. I can't make it alone! I talked to my mother yesterday, and she will be here in a few days to pick me up when I get discharged from the hospital. I'm returning to New York with her.

I wasn't on duty when Baby was discharged. I hope she accomplished her plan to go home with her mother to New York and get her life together. I also hope that she has achieved the healthy and happy life that she deserves.

Ghost of Scorned Woman Attacks Nurses!

I worked on the cardiac care step-down unit of a small hospital that I'll refer to as Regional Hospital. The building of this community hospital was completed around 1940, so the hospital had been in operation for almost seventy-eight years by the time I went to work there. This hospital was very haunted, and the ghosts there were very active. As soon as I entered the doors to this hospital on the day of my interview, I knew I would be dealing with a lot of spirits in this hospital—if I decided to take the job. However, I didn't have a clue as to how physical some of them might become. A few days later, I was officially offered the job, and I accepted it.

There were three halls on our unit, and I had worked only two of them for the first three months I was there. That changed as soon as we were "in season" and our patient population exploded. In case you are wondering what I mean by "in season," it refers to the time in which snow birds (people from up north) migrate to Florida to avoid the harsh winter. Season can begin as early as October and extend out to as late as the first of June. Anyway, the very haunted third hall had been closed to patient use for the summer and reopened in the fall. On the first day the hall was reopened, I was assigned an admission that was placed in room 361 on that hall.

My admission was a sweet 84 year old petite lady who was scheduled for a cardiac catheterization the next day. The emergency room nurses, Nancy and Margie, were already in the room with the patient when I got there. Nancy was tall and slender with blonde hair and green eyes. Margie was petite with short brown hair and brown eyes. As soon as I crossed the threshold of the door, I received a shove to my shoulders that sent me sprawling to the center of the room where I face-planted. The fall was so hard that the screen on my cell phone—which was in my scrub pocket—was shattered. I also received a nasty bruise to my left cheek. The two emergency room nurses ran to my side to make sure that I was okay. Margie asked Nancy what room we were in as if to make a point. Nancy looked up at Margie, and shaking her head she replied, "We're in the infamous room 361." Margie said, "Well, that explains it Lucy!"

They assessed me to make sure I didn't have any injuries before helping me get off the floor. Then they helped me get the patient settled into bed and oriented to the room. As the three of us walked out of the room together, I asked these two nurses what they meant by the "infamous room 361." They briefly looked at each and smiled. Then, they both looked at me and Nancy said, "You don't know about this room, do you?" I asked her to explain to me what she was talking about. She replied, "This room is haunted by a ghost who hates nurses. Ask one of the other nurses who have worked here for a while and they can tell you the story about the ghost who haunts this room."

I stood outside room 361 and watched as Nancy and Margie walked away down the hall towards the elevators. They were talking and laughing between themselves, which caused me to wonder what they were laughing about. Were they laughing because they had just sold me a bill of goods about the ghost or were they carrying on as usual. As I stood outside in the hallway, I asked God to fill me in on what was really happening in that room. This is what I was shown:

Immediately I started seeing visions of a scene out of the 1940's. I knew it had to be the the 1940's because of the clothing and hair styles I was seeing. I watched as a tall, full-figured woman with red hair, wearing a green dress pushed a petite woman with black hair who was wearing a nurse's uniform and cap to the floor. She started beating her brutally with her fists until the nurse's face was bloody. A soldier who was standing close by pulled the red-head off the nurse and shook her violently. He yelled at her, "It's over and there is nothing that you can do to make me love you again. I have moved on and so must you. I'm in love with Sandra and we are going to be married this Saturday. Stay away from us, or I swear I will make sure that something bad happens to you!"

I then watched as the red-head fell into a big black hole. I took this to mean that she had fallen into a deep, dark depression. I felt an intense sense of despair and anger coming from her that I have never perceived before, and I hope I never do again. I saw her trying to come out of the hole but not making it. Then I saw her lying in a hospital bed with bandages on both wrists. She looked older than she had looked during the fight—she had several streaks of gray hair and wrinkles around her mouth. This scene quickly morphed into the next scene where I saw her hanging by the neck from a pillow case tied to a hook in the hospital bathroom.

This woman had committed suicide in the bathroom of room 361. Now, her spirit was trapped there until someone could convince her to move on. After the shove she gave me, there was no way I was going to try to convince her to move on—she would just have to stay in hospital purgatory, unless I could get someone who was not a nurse to help move her on.

After this vision, I went to the staff lounge to take a minute to digest what I had just seen and try to brush off the negative aftershocks of my encounter with the angry spirit. When I entered the lounge, Rosa—the charge nurse—was sitting at the table with her head in her hands. It was no secret that her grown daughter had been giving her a lot of grief, running around doing drugs and abandoning her baby whom Rosa had to care for most of the time. She wearily looked up at me and said, "How's your day going." I told her that with the exception of falling on my face in room 361, it was going well. She cocked her head and glanced over at me with a puzzled look and asked, "What do you mean, falling on your face? What happened?" I told her what happened and that I was okay—the two E.D. nurses, Nancy and Margie, checked me out and I had no serious injuries. She told me that over the last twenty years she had worked on the unit, there have been many nurses assaulted in that room with several of them seriously hurt by an invisible assailant. She went on to tell me about the nurses who had received the worst injuries. These are the stories:

> Two years ago, a nurse got her nose broken when she entered that room. Some invisible force smacked her across the face sending her backwards on her butt. The patient in that room saw the whole thing happen and

demanded to be moved out of the haunted room immediately. He said he had never seen anything like it before. He could see her nose being pushed in and bloodied, but there was nothing there to cause it—except for maybe a ghost. He said he never believed in ghost before, but he definitely does now. We wasted no time in moving him to another room. The nurse was sent to the E.D. where they tried to set her badly broken nose. She was out of work for a couple of weeks before coming back on the condition that she never had to enter that room again. Of course, we honored her request.

Five years ago, a nurse who was doing some bedside teaching on the patient's upcoming procedure started coughing and choking mid-sentence. According to the patient, she grabbed her throat as if she was trying to pull invisible hands off of her. She continued struggling to breathe until she fell to the floor. The patient said that he pushed the nurse call button the moment she started having trouble breathing, but it took a while for someone to answer. By the time the unit secretary answered the light and sent a CNA into the room, the nurse had already stopped breathing. When the CNA entered the room and saw the nurse lying on the floor unresponsive, she called the secretary and told her to call a code. The code team arrived shocked to see it was the nurse that needed to be resuscitated, not the patient.

By this time, the nurse was now in complete respiratory and cardiac arrest—no respirations or pulse. Within five minutes, the team was able to bring her back and send her to the critical care unit where she made a full recovery. Her doctors and nurses were shocked to hear that she had never had a history of asthma or any other obstructive type respiratory disease. She said she wasn't chewing on gum or anything else that would cause her to choke when the attack happened. In her heart, she knew she had been attacked by a ghost, but how could she convince her healthcare providers that that's what happened so that they would stop all the respiratory testing. She just wanted to get home to her family and put the whole incident behind her. While she was still in the ICU, she had her husband submit her resignation letter. In the letter, she stated that she never wanted to be exposed again to whatever caused her death on our unit.

About eight years ago, we had a nurse who fell and broke her ankle in that room. She said she was walking at a normal pace, and something tripped her causing her to fall. There was nothing on the floor to cause her to trip, nor was the floor wet. The patient witnessed the fall and said he saw what looked like a white mist swirling around her feet and lower legs when she fell. He said he shook his head and the mist was still there, but it disappeared after the fall. He also said he thought the room was haunted because the first night he was hospitalized, he saw a tall woman with red hair and a malevolent grin on her face standing in the bathroom. At first he thought she was a physical lady until she faded and disappeared from his sight. He said he hadn't seen her again since then and didn't think too much more about it because he acknowledged the possibility that the whole hospital may be very haunted.

Three months later, after convalescing from ankle surgery, the nurse returned to work, but she refused to go back to the cardiac step-down unit. Instead, she went to work in the cardiac intensive care unit where she could decrease the amount of required walking she would have to do. Her ankle was healed but would swell anytime she was on her feet for an extended amount of time. She had only a couple of years left before she could retire, and she was determined to hang in there until then. Unfortunately, when she did retire, she enjoyed about six months of it before she was diagnosed with cancer and died a year later.

Later that evening at home, I got to thinking about the vision I had earlier that day. As I was thinking about my first vision, I had a second one. In my second vision I witnessed a scene where this soldier was in a hospital bed and his nurse was the same one I saw in the first vision. While this nurse was at the soldier's bedside, the redheaded woman came into the room and gave the soldier a big hug and kiss. She started talking about plans for their wedding, and he said he didn't care what kind of wedding they had as long as they got married soon. Of course, that never happened, because he married the nurse. The redheaded woman I saw in my first vision was definitely a woman scorned. She was utterly devastated by the broken promise of marriage to this WWII soldier.

During WWII, there was an air-force base located about five blocks away from the hospital where these ghostly attacks took place. The army completely abandoned this air force base in 1946. There was also a military hospital in the center of town—probably the hospital where this GI Joe met the nurse he married instead of the redhead. My point is that my visions made a lot of sense because the hospital where this redheaded ghost attacks nurses is located in a town that was a major military hub during WWII. My heart goes out to the ghost of this redheaded woman who was scorned, but I wish she would stop attacking innocent nurses who had nothing to do with her broken heart. I didn't try to reason with her to help her move on because she is so angry towards nurses, she would have never listened to me. Hopefully, one day a male medium will come along and convince her to cross over.

Ghost Nuns Still Provide Good Help!

At the time I worked on the cardiac care step-down unit of this hospital, I had no knowledge that Nuns had owned and operated it several years before. Every evening on my way out of the hospital to go home, I passed the administrative offices. On one particular evening as I was approaching the main door to theses offices, a nun who looked to be in her thirties walked out of the door, stopped, and nodded at me before continuing down the hall in front of me. She wasn't wearing the traditional habit, wimple, and veil. She wore what looked like a dark gray, below-the-knee length cotton skirt with a light gray cotton turtle neck shirt, and beige colored stockings. On her head she wore a short gray veil with a white band around the front edge. Around her neck was a silver crucifix on a long silver chain that hung loosely over her chest. She carried a brown leather briefcase in her right hand and a black purse on her left shoulder. I followed her all the way to the front lobby where she faded out of sight before ever reaching the front doors. Until she faded from my sight, I thought she was a regular physical person—she was just that solid!

The next day at work, I told the charge nurse, Linda, about the nun I had seen the evening before and asked her if nuns had ever worked at this hospital. She said that a group of nuns had owned and operated the hospital for twenty-nine years. They purchased it in 1985, and sold it in 2014. While their stated objective was to care for patients from all socio-economic groups, in some territories they operated for-profit private hospitals. Their motto was "Good Help to Those in Need."

Linda went on to say that after the sisters sold the hospital, both employees and visitors had reported seeing nuns in the hospital. When the nuns operated the hospital, they didn't work as bedside nurses; they worked in positions of authority such as charge nurse, nurse manager, director of nursing and administrator. Lay nurses were hired to provide direct patient care. However, the nuns were very loving and involved in making sure that all their patients had a positive hospital experience while receiving excellent care. Although the charge nurses were not necessarily hands on, they would make patient rounds to ensure the patients were getting what they needed. They often tucked patients into bed or straightened their bedcovers. I think our patients received much better care when the nuns managed the hospital. I wish they were still running things.

I told Linda I believed the ghosts of some of the nuns who had worked at this hospital were still trying to help run things—that they come and go from heaven to accomplish various missions as needed. For example, the ghosts of nuns who worked in administration when they were alive, may continue to work in administration. Their work, however, in the afterlife may be to pray for and influence the minds of the current administrators so they will create the best policies for patient care. For those nuns who were charge nurses, their ghosts may continue to provide for the comfort of the patients by tucking them into bed. Linda shifted in her chair, leaned forward and said that it wasn't uncommon for a patient to say something to the effect of, "I didn't know nuns still worked here. One came into my room and tucked my bedcovers last night." Our discussion was interrupted by an overhead page for Linda to go to the nurse's station. Before she left the staff lounge, she suggested that we have lunch together that day so she could tell me about the time she saw a nun walking down the hall and entering a patient's room.

I met up with Linda at one o'clock for lunch in the staff lounge. Several other nurses were already sitting at the table and talking amongst themselves when we entered together. We got our lunches and sat down at the table. Linda didn't waste anytime in starting her story. The other two nurses sitting at the table became quiet and gave Linda their full attention. This is the story Linda told us in the lounge that day:

We were experiencing a nurse staffing shortage on the night shift, so I agreed to work a few nights to help out. I am not a night person, and I have a hard time staying awake sometimes. When I start feeling overwhelmed by sleepiness, I'll take a walk to try to wake up. On the night I saw the ghost nun, I was taking a walk to shake off the grogginess I was feeling. As I entered the hallway from the nurse's station, I saw the backside of a nun wearing a navy blue dress with the hem below the knees and a short veil on her head. She was about halfway down the hall, and I watched as she went into a patient's room on the left. I followed her into that room, and—of course the room was empty—no one was there. I turned around and walked out of that room when I saw her in the patient's room across the hall. I stood by the door of that room and watched her. She was bent over an elderly male patient's bed and straightening his covers. She stood up, turned around, looked at me and smiled before disappearing into thin air. Her face was as radiant as the sun, and she had a bluish-white halo around her head. I stood outside the room for a moment pinching myself to wake from my dream, but is wasn't a dream. I felt every pinch that I made and later on had the bruises on my arms to prove my experience was real.

I walked back up to the nurses' station and told the nurses about my experience. Sandy, one of the nurses who had worked the night shift on this unit for the last twenty years said, "Oh, you saw Mary. She was a nun who worked nights as a charge nurse on this unit when the Sisters were still here. She died from ovarian cancer a couple of years before they sold the hospital." That was the last time I saw Mary. I never agreed to work the night shift again.

Susan one of the other nurses sitting at the table

chimed in and started talking about her encounter with Mary. Susan worked the night shift until an opening came available on the day shift and she moved into that position. This is her story:

> I would see Mary walk in and out of rooms all the time when I worked the night shift. When the CNA's took the six a.m. vitals every morning, patients would frequently ask them who the nun was that came into their room during the night. They always appeared shocked when they were told that we didn't have nuns working with us anymore. Sometimes, our patients would wake up during the night to see Mary straightening their covers, or holding their hand. Some patients reported seeing a nun with rosary beads who was kneeling beside their bed praying.

Although the thought of having a ghost in your room can be downright scary, it can also be comforting to know that the spirit of a nun is intervening in your healing and healthcare through their prayers and presence. I welcome the presence of the ghost nuns, and I hope they will continue to intervene by providing therapeutic touch, comfort measures, and prayer for us and our patients for as long as this hospital remains in business.

~ Six ~

HAUNTED HOSPITAL ROOMS

"Death is no more than passing from one room into another."

— Helen Keller

Mr. Claws—The Ghost With Metal Hands

When I worked on the medical-surgical unit at Jay Hospital, we had a haunted private patient room at the very end of the medical hall—room 214, which was actually room 213. We were constantly having to move patients out of this room because after spending just one night in that room, many patients demanded to be moved the next morning. Paranormal activity got so bad we finally had to close it as a patient room and turn it into a storage room. Out of all the patient complaints I received about this room being haunted, there were two that literally scared the hell out of me—the encounters Jessica and David had with the ghost of Mr. Claws.

Jessica's Encounter With Mr. Claws

Jessica was a 24-year-old woman who was admitted with a diagnosis of renal calculi, which is the medical term for kidney stones. If you've ever been unfortunate enough to have kidney stones, you know it is a very painful condition and requires strong pain medications such as IV morphine. Morphine has been known to cause hallucinations, but Jessica swears she was not hallucinating during the night when she saw the man with the metal claws standing in her bathroom. One of the symptoms of kidney stones is the persistent urge to urinate; needless to say Jessica made several trips to the bathroom throughout the night of her admission. All of her trips to the bathroom were uneventful except for one.

Around four o'clock in the morning when she got up to urinate in the hat (a receptacle that fits under the toilet lid and collects urine and/or feces), she opened the bathroom door to find a ghost dressed in a flannel shirt and bib coveralls standing by the sink. When she got a closer look at him, she noticed his hands were actually metal claws. Before she could move, he was in her face and shoving his claws into her right lower abdomen. She peed herself and fell backwards slipping in her urine. She screamed and several staff members came running into the room. They turned on the light and found her sitting on the floor by the bathroom door in a puddle of pee. She was hysterical and sobbing inconsolably. The nurses assessed her for injuries and then helped her get cleaned up and back to bed. She demanded they move her out of that room immediately, but no other rooms were available until the next morning after discharges. She told them if they couldn't move her, she would go home against medical advice. Once they got her back to bed, she was hurting so bad she doubled over and screamed at the nurse to get her more morphine. Within several minutes after getting the morphine, she fell sound asleep and slept until I entered her room about seven-thirty that morning.

As soon as I walked into Jessica's room, she wasted no time in telling me about her encounter with the ghost she sarcastically referred to as Mr. Claws. She asked me if I believed her story, and I told her the hospital was very old and it was possible it could be haunted. What I didn't tell her was I had also seen Mr. Claws and so had several other patients who had stayed in that room. As I stood by her bed with my back to the open bathroom door, I could sense him watching us. Jessica demanded that I move her immediately or she would just get up and leave the hospital. I assured her I would have her moved to another room that morning as soon as I discharged some patients.

Around ten o'clock, a room became available and I had Jessica transferred to it within thirty minutes. As soon as we got her settled, she made me promise that if the new room was haunted, I would immediately move her to one that wasn't haunted, even if it was on another floor. I finally broke down and told her that I was a psychic medium, and if her new room was haunted, I would know about it. I convinced her that the new room was not haunted and she would be safe. Because Jessica hadn't passed the kidney stones, her doctor scheduled her to have a lithotripsy to crush and remove them the next morning. I did her preoperative teaching and told her what to expect just before, during and after the procedure, but I didn't tell her about the elderly female ghost who haunts the post-op unit. Many patients have seen her standing by their gurney as they were waking up from anesthesia. She has been described as a sweet, gray haired grandmother in a patient gown with round wire-rim glasses and a big smile. I was off duty for the next few days and Jessica was discharged before I returned to work, so I wasn't able to follow up with her to find out if she encountered the elderly female ghost while she was recovering in post-op. Anyway, it was my hope at the time that the doctor would be able to crush and remove all of her kidney stones so she wouldn't have to spend another night in a hospital anytime soon.

David's Encounter With Mr. Claws

David was a forty-year-old diabetic patient admitted to room 214 with a diagnosis of gangrene of the left great toe. Attempts to save his toe with silvadene dressing changes and IV antibiotics had failed. He was now scheduled to have his toe amputated the next day. David had been a brittle diabetic from childhood and feared that one day he would start losing limbs. Although he wasn't losing a limb, he believed losing his left great toe was a precursor of things to soon come. That is why when he encountered Mr. Claws on the night of his admission, he thought maybe he was having a prophetic dream confirming his fear of future amputations.

The next morning around seven-thirty, I hung his pre-operative antibiotic and prepared him to go down to surgery. I asked David if he had any questions or concerns. He said he knew what to expect and really didn't have any questions, but he was anxious about the surgery because he had a bad dream during the night. I asked him if he wanted to talk about it. He said he thought he might feel a lot better if he could tell someone about it because it was so disturbing. He took a deep breath and blew it out, then proceeded to tell his dream to me. This is what he said:

> My dream started when I returned to bed after going to the bathroom about two o'clock this morning. No sooner had I closed my eyes, when I saw a man who was dressed like a farmer with a flannel shirt, bib coveralls, and a wide brim hat standing at the foot of my bed. He had big black holes where his eyes and mouth should have been. I looked down and noticed that this farmer didn't have normal fingers but metal fingers that looked like claws. I could feel the cold, sharp metal of his claws as he tried to tear my feet away from my ankles. I was horrified and couldn't move or yell out for help. He continued ripping at my feet with his claws until my feet were completely severed from my ankles.

With a tone of despair, David stated he hoped the dream didn't mean that he was going to wake up from surgery with both feet amputated. I reassured him that before he received anesthesia, he would participate with the surgeon and O.R. team in identifying what was to be removed during surgery. I also told him the consent he signed gave the surgeon permission to remove only his left great toe and nothing else. What I didn't tell him was that his room was haunted by Mr. Claws and that he wasn't the first to encounter this ghost. After surgery he would be coming back to the same room, and I wasn't about to put more fear in him than he was already experiencing.

David's surgery went well, and he returned to room 214 later that afternoon. Although he was experiencing intense pain, he seemed to be in a good mood. I commented that he must be feeling better now the surgery was over. He said he was just relieved to wake up with both feet connected to the ankle. I mentioned that the dream must have really unnerved him. He said it was the worst nightmare he ever remembered having. What he didn't know at the time was that his worst nightmare was yet to come.

I had David as a patient again the next day and his mood had completely changed. As soon as I walked into his room at seven-thirty in the morning, he yelled at me and asked why his fucking toe hurt so bad. I asked him if had been pressing his PCA button when he feels pain. He said he had pressed that damn button non-stop. I checked the PCA settings and the medication seemed to be dispensing correctly as ordered. I told him I would talk to the doctor about getting an order to increase his pain medication. I also told him that watching t.v., doing a cross word puzzle, or reading a book could be helpful in decreasing the perception of pain. He started crying and apologized for yelling at me. He told me he had another nightmare, which was much worse than the one he had the previous night.

In this nightmare, he said he was lying on a table in a barn while the farmer ripped away his arms and legs and replaced them with claws. He said he woke up with the feeling that he had just had another prophetic dream that someday he would lose all of his extremities. I asked him why he believed the dream was prophetic. He said that he had always known that one day he would lose his extremities to diabetes and that the dream confirmed it. I told David the only thing the dream confirmed was his fear. I knew then that the ghost of Mr. Claws was definitely an evil entity seeking to play upon the fears of his victims. Apparently he got an energetic charge from their fears, which fueled his miserable existence. I couldn't hold back any longer; I had to tell David about the ghost haunting his room.

I took a deep breath and sighed. David asked me what was wrong. I blurted out that he wasn't the first patient to see the farmer with claws. He sat up in bed, looked at me sternly and asked me what I meant. I told him that the patient who had been in the room before him had seen Mr. Claws too. He cocked his head to the side and asked me to explain what I was talking about. I told him that another patient had seen Mr. Claws standing in the bathroom. He asked me if I was trying to say the room was haunted and why I would knowingly put him in a haunted room. I told him I didn't have any control over patient room assignments, and that the hospital was very old and probably had many haunted rooms. He yelled at me to move him to another room immediately or he would sign himself out. I told him I would try to get him moved within an hour.

After talking to the charge nurse, I was able to get a room for him on another hall on our unit. As promised, with the help of my CNA, I had him moved within an hour. David was assigned to another nurse on the new hall for the rest of the shift. I worked the next day, but I didn't have him as a patient. I stopped by the next morning to see him before he was discharged to go home. He said he had a peaceful night's sleep with no sign of the farmer in his dreams. I told him to keep the faith and believe for good outcomes. In the years I worked on this unit, David never returned as a patient. Hopefully, he was able to stay well and didn't need our services. I can't say as I blame him if he chose not to be a patient in our haunted hospital again.

I talked to a couple of nurses who had worked at the hospital for at least ten years about Mr. Claws. These nurses remembered taking care of a patient in room 214 who had metal prosthesis on both lower arms. He was a farmer who lost both hands in a chipping machine accident. During his hospitalization, he fell in the bathroom, hitting his head on the sink. He sustained a fractured skull and had emergency surgery to remove splintered bone fragments and relieve pressure from intracranial swelling. Unfortunately he didn't make it—he died in surgery. It's a shame because his death could have been avoided if he had only called for assistance, but he was a proud and independent man who refused to ask for help.

The Ghost of Post-Op Granny

Not all encounters with ghosts are horrifying, some can be very comforting. I have taken care of several post surgical patients who reported being awakened in post-op cubicle #7 by a patient who looked like a kindly grandma. They always described her as a sweet, gray haired lady in a patient gown with round wire-rim glasses and a big smile who tucked in their covers and touched their wounds.

Judy's Encounter With Post-Op Granny

I had Judy as a patient on the ob/gyn unit of Jay Hospital. She was a 38 year old woman who had undergone a myomectomy to treat uterine fibroids a year earlier. Unfortunately, the fibroids grew back causing her more pain and bleeding than she had before the procedure. Now she was hemorrhaging and had to have an emergency hysterectomy to completely remove her uterus. I admitted Judy to the unit before her hysterectomy and prepped her to go down for surgery. (These days, many patients are not admitted to the floor until they have had their surgery because a lot of patients go home afterwards.) Although she was relieved that her ordeal with the constant bleeding would soon be over, understandably, she was very apprehensive about going under the knife. Her surgery went well and she was recovered in post-op bed #7.

Judy returned to the floor in a obtunded state of consciousness, mumbling something about the grandma who tucked her in. Within a couple of hours, she was completely awake and in significant pain. I reminded her to use her PCA (patient controlled analgesia), which helped to ease her pain. As I was checking her perineal pad, she told me that a patient who looked like somebody's grandma massaged her tummy and said that everything would be okay. I asked her what this grandma looked like, and she said she was in a white patient gown, had gray hair pulled back into a bun, and wore round, wire rim glasses. I apologized that the staff was apparently unable to keep this grandma patient from wandering into her cubicle. I told her I couldn't understand how it could happen because usually the post-op nurse is very close by. This was the first report I received from a patient about the ghost of post-op granny. Of course, I knew her experience wasn't related to the side effects of the anesthetic or analgesic drugs she had received because the grandma ghost made herself known to me in a vision before Judy told me her story.

Rick's Encounter With Post-Op Granny

Rick was a forty-five year old patient of mine who had a laparoscopic cholecystectomy (lap chole), a surgery in which the gallbladder is removed through several small cuts instead of one large one. He had issues with labile heart rates and blood pressures along with excessive pain, so the surgeon admitted him to twenty-four hour observation on our medical-surgical unit. According to the report I received from the post-op nurse, Rick took much longer than most patients to wake up. Once he was awake, his heart rate escalated to 120 beats per minute and his blood pressure spiked to 240/110. Apparently, he had experienced an episode of cardiac baroreflex, which can occur in post-op patients with preexisting hypertension. They gave him IV clonidine, which helped to decrease his heart rate and blood pressure. As soon as he was stabilized, they sent him to the floor under my care.

When I received Rick to the floor, he was wide awake and gregarious. He said if he had to stay in the hospital he was glad to have such a pretty nurse to look at. He was quite the flirt! He carried on with me a few more minutes before he became silent. With a serious look on his face, he said he had the weirdest dream while in was in the recovery room. He dreamed of this sweet old lady with round, wire rim glasses and gray hair pulled back into a bun. She touched his head and stomach and with a smile on her face said that everything was going to be okay. The next thing he said he remembered was the nurse calling his name trying to get him to wake up.

Rick stayed overnight, and his heart rate and blood pressure remained stable. I discharged him to home the next day. After I gave him his discharge instructions, I asked him if he had any questions. He said, "No, but if you happen to see grandma downstairs, tell her thanks for the healing boost." Our eyes connected and he looked at me with a crooked smile on his face and a twinkle in he eye as if to say he knew that his dream wasn't a dream at all, but an encounter with a healing ghost.

In the weeks following Rick's discharge, I had the opportunity to speak with several of the post-op nurses while receiving patient reports from them over the phone. I told them about the experience two of my patients had and asked them if they had any patients that reported seeing the granny ghost. Every nurse I spoke with said they knew about the granny ghost and that she was harmless. Two of the nurses said they had seen her full apparition standing in post-op cubicle #7. Other nurses said they knew when she was close by because they could feel her warmth and loving presence. No one seemed to know who she was or how she died, but they all agreed they loved having her around.

The Supply Room Poltergeists

About ten years before I started working on the medical-surgical unit at Jay Hospital, room 201 had been a private patient room. Paranormal activity had become so bad in that room they could no longer use it as a patient room, so it was converted into a supply room. The story goes that the call bell light would go on and off even when the room was empty. When it was occupied, patients would become frustrated at the constant interruption from the unit secretary when they had not called for help. The bathroom light and emergency call light would constantly go on and off, and the bathroom door would open and close for no reason. No one ever recalled seeing an apparition in that room, but the staff believed that it was definitely haunted.

Hospital maintenance and outside contractors had

been called in several times to try and trouble shoot the call bell system, but never found any problems with it. The system always worked correctly when they tested it. Once room 201 was converted to a supply room, the activity became worse. The frequency of the call light coming on increased to the point that it became necessary to disconnect the call button cord from the wall and mute the beep on the call light box at the nurses station. The bathroom door had to be padlocked to keep it from opening and slamming shut.

By the time I started working as a nurse on this unit, it was a regular occurrence to actually witness supplies being thrown off the metal racks and scattered all over the floor as if by invisible hands. Several nurses, including myself, have been in the supply room at the same time and watched as several boxes of gauze levitated and flew off the shelf. Exterminators frequently inspected the supply room and never found any mice or rats, so there was no explanation for this activity other than the room was haunted by a poltergeist. I asked my highest guide, Yeshua, who was haunting the supply room. I was shown two visions—the first was of an elderly lady who appeared to have dementia and the second one was of a young woman who was extremely angry.

The elderly lady in my vision was very petite—about five feet tall—and had short white hair with curls like an old fashioned baby doll. Her face was round and her eyes were steel blue; she had a snub nose and a mole on her right cheek. She appeared to be suffering from some type of dementia as she wandered around her room picking things up and putting them down again. After roaming around the room for awhile, she would wander in and out of the bathroom pulling the emergency string and causing staff members to come running to her rescue. Nurses would help her back into bed, gently tucking her in while explaining to her that it was nap time. As soon as they left the room, she would start playing with the nurse call button and t.v. remote control. After a few minutes of pressing the buttons, she would get out of bed and start roaming again.

I asked Spirit why she was in the hospital, and I was told that she had a severe urinary tract infection and required intravenous antibiotics. I looked at her right lower arm and saw that it had Kling gauze wrapped around it, which was apparently applied to deter her from pulling her I.V. out. I was shown that she was restrained with wrist restraints bilaterally only while she was receiving her I.V. antibiotic, otherwise she wasn't restrained. When the infusion was over, the nurse removed the wrist restraints. As soon as the nurse left the room, she got out of bed, went into the bathroom and turned the water on at the sink. I watched as the sink overflowed spilling water out onto the floor. She turned around and started to walk away when she slipped on the puddle of water, fell backwards and hit her head on the sink. A staff member who was out in the hallway near the door to her room heard her fall and came running in. What he saw when he entered the bathroom was a gruesome scene out of a nightmare. She had hit her head so hard that it crushed her skull. When she fell to the floor splintered bone fragments, brain matter, and blood splattered on the walls. I understood why she was haunting room 201. She was in the same state of demented consciousness she was in before she died suddenly and tragically. She was earthbound because she was oblivious to the light.

The young woman that I saw in my second vision looked to be in her mid-twenties. She was about five feet, six inches tall and slender with shoulder length brown hair, hazel eyes, and a slightly hooked nose. Her face was badly bruised and swollen, and her bottom lip was split open. She had a cervical collar around her neck and a binder around her ribs. I watched as she sat in bed crying and throwing things across the room. I asked Spirit to show me why she was so upset. I was told that her husband had been out drinking and ended up sleeping with another woman all night long. I was shown a scene where she confronted him the next morning over his whereabouts the previous night. He became extremely violent and started beating her in the head, ribs, and gut. He even picked her up by the arms and threw her across the room a couple of times. My heart went out to her as tears streamed down my cheeks. I could feel the love she had for this man along with a sense of betrayal by him. She was inconsolable.

I was then shown a scene where she was hoarding her pain pills. She pretended to swallow them when the nurse gave them to her, but as soon as the nurse left the room, she would spit them out and put them in a pouch she kept in the drawer of the bedside table. One night after the nurse gave her more pain medication and the CNA took her last set of vital signs for the night, the young woman opened the bedside table drawer, pulled out the pain meds she had been hoarding and washed them all down with the water the nurse left at the bedside. She turned out the lights, pulled the covers up to her neck and went to sleep for the last time. By the time the CNA rounded on her at six o'clock the next morning to take her vital signs, she had been dead for several hours from the overdose and rigor mortis had already set in. She committed suicide in room 201, and her angry spirit was still there because she couldn't see the light.

That evening at home I decided I would try to cross these two spirits over the next day at work. I planned to go in thirty minutes before the start of my shift so that I would have time to communicate with them and convince them to go. That night before I went to bed, I put on my cross necklace and packed holy water and several of my favorite small crystals for protection in my nursing bag, which normally only contained my stethoscope, hemostat, pen light, and bandage scissors. My favorite crystals for protection, which I sometimes use in combination, are black tourmaline, jet, smoky quartz, and amethyst. Black tourmaline is a powerful stone for protection and is the best crystal for repelling lower energies and frequencies. The reason black tourmaline is so effective is that it transmutes negative energy into positive, and acts as a metaphysical force field around you, to keep other people's bad thoughts and feelings away. Jet protects against violence, illness, dark entities, and spirit attachments. Smoky quartz is unlimited in transmuting negative energy and is a must have for spiritual or psychic protection. It dissolves negative energy fields caused by thoughts such as anger and resentment and grounds them back to earth. It has a gentle essence, but is a powerful protective stone. If you do any kind of work with the spirit realm, such as mediumship or paranormal investigation, crystals can provide you with protection from detrimental forces. Amethyst is one of the most spiritual stones. Its high vibration will protect your energy field against psychic attack and negativity. Like smoky quartz, amethyst is a powerful protection stone for transmuting negative energy into positive. An important principle to understand when working with crystals is that they are only as effective as you believe them to be! Faith is the most important ingredient in any type of spiritual work.

I said prayers of protection during my entire drive to work the next day, not because I was afraid of the two poltergeists, but because I knew I could inadvertently draw the attention of many other spirits I wouldn't necessarily be able to deal with at the same time. As you may realize by now, hospitals are full of spirits. Once I was parked in the staff parking lot, I placed all four stones into my right scrub pocket and took a deep breath before making the trek in the icy cold air of winter to the back entrance to the hospital.

I had arrived thirty minutes early as planned and went straight to the supply room. Before I entered the door to the supply room, I pulled out my holy water and made the sign of the cross on the door jam and door. Once I had entered the room, I anointed the door jam and door on the other side. I walked into the center of the room and called out the spirit of the confused elderly lady. She was standing in the far right hand corner and turned around to look at me. Within a few seconds, she was no further than one inch from my face. It startled me so bad that I stumbled backwards hitting one of the metal racks behind me. I don't think she was trying to scare me, but she was just very confused and didn't know how to interact with me appropriately. I knew I wouldn't be able to reason with her, so I created a portal to heaven in my mind and asked God to send her loved ones in spirit and Michael the Archangel to come forward and escort her to heaven. No sooner than I had made my request, her husband, mother, and father accompanied by St. Michael showed up and crossed her over. I didn't have to say a word to her. She didn't even look back. The portal closed and I breathed a sigh of relief that she was gone.

Unfortunately, I didn't have the same success with her ghosty roommate. The young female ghost wouldn't even acknowledge me when I spoke to her. She just started throwing supplies off the metal racks. I said a prayer that God would send angels to rescue her and take her to heaven someday. I picked up my nursing bag, put the stones back in it and took my stethoscope out and placed it around my neck. I walked over to the door, and as I reached for the handle, the poltergeist activity stopped. I remember thinking to myself that she knew I was there, but wouldn't communicate with me because she didn't want to cross over. It occurred to me as I walked out the door, that I wasn't only a nurse for the living, but a nurse for the dead as well. I walked into the supply room that morning as a nurse providing spirit rescue for my ghost patients and walked out as nurse providing medical-surgical care for my living patients. Now, I had the tools that I needed for my dead and living patients. I decided that the stones would stay in my nursing bag as part of my arsenal of necessary work tools.

~ Seven ~

PATIENT ENCOUNTERS
WITH THE DEAD

"I like to say I believe in ghosts so I don't get haunted by one."

—Ella Henderson

Glimpses of the Afterlife

Over the years in my career as a nurse, I have received many reports from my patients about their encounters with the dead during near death experiences, death bed visions, and dream visitations. Most of these reports came from patients who were in the process of dying; some had died and come back after being resuscitated; and a few had just awakened from a dream. In the section of this chapter entitled *Dream Visitations*, I will recount some of the dream visitations my patients shared with me. In the section entitled *Near Death Experiences*, I will discuss the near death experiences my patients told me about. Finally, in the section entitled *Deathbed Visions*, I will describe the most intriguing deathbed visions my dying patients had. But first, I would like to give you a brief glimpse into the afterlife as it pertains to the three aforementioned types of encounters with the world of the dead.

Dreams are considered one of the most effective ways for spirits to connect with the living. Spirits communicate with us while we are asleep because we're more likely to be receptive to them in a dream than we would be if we were awake. These dreams are called visitation dreams. Visitation dreams are typically vivid, have a linear progression of events, contain a core message, and are always remembered upon awakening. These dreams are so real you wake up feeling that you have actually interacted with the spirit of the deceased person you dreamed about. Spirits attempt to convey messages in dreams for any number of reasons, but usually it's because they want to provide comfort, guidance, or a warning.

Many people who have talked about their near death experience (also known as a NDE) said they had the sensation of floating up towards the ceiling and could see their body below. They were also able to view the activities of all the people in their room before entering a tunnel of light. Not all people entered a tunnel, but those who did and had a positive experience said they remembered spending time in a beautiful, otherworldly realm where they met deceased loved ones, friends, angels and a loving, warm presence they referred to as God. They said it felt like they were connected to all creation while on the other side. Some recalled having a life review, but it wasn't a judgmental experience. One of the most significant characteristics of near death experiences that all NDEers (people who have had a near death experience) seem to agree upon is that they perceived the afterlife as being even more real than physical life. They did not feel as though they were having a hallucination or a dream. While most NDEs are positive, there are some that are negative.

Close to the moment of death, apparitions of deceased friends, loved ones, and/or angels appear to escort the dying to the other side. Such deathbed visions are not just the stuff of ghost stories and paranormal movies. They are more common than you might think and are surprisingly similar across nationalities, religions, and cultures. Exactly how many people experience deathbed visions is difficult to ascertain because only about ten percent of dying people are conscious shortly before death. Of this ten percent, it is estimated that between fifty and sixty percent of patients experience deathbed visions. Most of these visions seem to last about five minutes and are mostly seen by people who approach death gradually, such as those suffering from a terminal illness or a life-threatening injury. Instances of deathbed visions have been recorded throughout history and stand as one of the most compelling proofs of life after death.

Dream Visitations

In dream visitations, the deceased usually appear much younger and healthier than when they died. The messages conveyed by the deceased in these dreams always seem to center around giving hope and reassurance to the dreamer. The dream structure is typically clear, vivid, intense, and is experienced as a real visit when the dreamer awakens. Most of the time, the dreamer is changed in some beneficial way by the experience. The following stories of Faith and Sarah demonstrate the powerful impact these dream visitations can have.

Faith is Visited by her Dead Mom

Faith was a 45 year old patient of mine who was admitted to the hospital to have a lobectomy of her left lung. She had been diagnosed with lung cancer two days earlier when the biopsy from a large tumor in her left lower lobe came back positive for oat cell carcinoma. She cried almost constantly, questioning why she had lung cancer since she had never smoked or done anything that would cause her to have lung cancer. She said she had always tried to take care of her health by getting proper exercise and not drinking or smoking.

I walked into her room early one morning while she was sitting up in bed eating breakfast with the t.v. on. At this point in her hospitalization, she had undergone the lobectomy surgery a week earlier and had the last chest tube removed the day before. She wasn't crying this morning as she did the previous two mornings. Instead, she greeted me with a smile on her face when I walked in and told me she wanted to share a dream with me because she knew I would understand. This is the dream she shared with me:

My mother who died from a heart attack twenty-five years ago came to me in a dream last night. She was healthy and looked like she was in her early thirties, like she did when I was a little girl. She was wearing her favorite outfit—a teal colored sundress, white sandals and a yellow straw purse that she carried in her left hand. She was surrounded by a bluish-white light that seemed to emanate the love she had for me. She told me she was well and enjoying her life in heaven with my dad and other loved ones, including Danny, my brother who died when he was nine years old. She said for me not to worry, that everything would work out okay and I would live a healthy life for many more years to come. She implored me to be happy and enjoy my life. As my mother turned and walked away, I felt a light breeze rush across me, from my left to my right and then I heard her say, "Faith, how many times have I told you to trust in the Lord."

I immediately woke from the dream and could smell her favorite perfume, "White Linen" in my room. Whenever I went through trials and tribulations in life, my mother, when alive, would always tell me to trust in the Lord. It was so comforting to hear her say those words. It was as if she was actually with me once again, cheering me on as she always did.

Tears streamed down my face as she described her dream. I told her I was very happy her mother came to her to reassure her that she would heal and live a healthy life for many years to come. I never saw her cry again. She always had a smile on her face and constantly talked about her plans for the future. Two days later, Faith was discharged to home with an excellent prognosis. It's amazing what having belief and trust in the Lord can do. It's called faith. Ironically, Faith's name, which has its root in the latin—*fides*, means complete trust and belief in God.

Sarah is Visited by her Dead Grandma

Sarah was a 35 year old patient of mine who had undergone a right mastectomy five days earlier. The surgeon felt that he removed all of the cancer, but she still had a large amount of lymphedema, which was a cause for concern. She would have to remain in the hospital until we could get the swelling under control. On the first day I had Sarah as a patient, she shared a dream with me that I will never forget.

As soon as I walked into her room that morning, she wasted no time in telling me that she had to be discharged immediately because she no longer had cancer and her grandma had just died—she needed to be with the family. She definitely caught me off guard with her comments. I looked at her and calmly stated that I understood why she felt the need to be with her family at such a time. But, she had to take care of herself too. I reminded her that she was still in the hospital because of the large amount of swelling in her arm, which could compromise circulation and lead to tissue death, and ultimately a loss of limb.

She glared at me with a stern look on her face and adamantly said, "I am going to leave today if it means that I just walk out! My grandma who just died came to me in a dream and said that the cancer is gone and I am going to live a long wonderful life."

Reflexively, I echoed back to her, "Your grandma who just died came to you in a dream?"

She replied, "Yes, she came to me in a dream and I think you need to hear it!" In a somewhat irritated tone of voice, she proceeded to tell me her dream:

In my dream, I heard my name being called very clearly, "Sarah, Sarah." It was a woman's voice that sounded like my maternal grandma, Betsy. It echoed behind me as if it was coming from a long hollow tunnel. I turned around and saw my grandma lying in a hospital bed. Her eyes were closed and her breathing was very labored. It occurred to me that she was in the process of dying. I looked to my left and glanced up at corner of the ceiling. There was a white light, which emanated a mist that looked like fog. I glanced back over at my grandma and a white mist rose from her body and glided towards the light. She called my name once again and asked if I was going to escort her into heaven. I began to feel the warmth and love emanating from the light and was overcome by an overwhelming compulsion to walk into it with my grandma. I knew that everything would be okay—there was nothing to fear in the light.

I seemed to glide over to my grandma who was standing at the entrance to the light. She extended her left hand towards me and I took it into mine. As we entered the light, I felt a sense of love and belonging much greater than anything that I had ever experienced before. We continued in the light through what appeared to be a tunnel until we reached a lush, green meadow. This meadow was filled with beautiful wildflowers of all types and colors. I could smell a bouquet of my favorite fragrances such as jasmine, cherry blossoms, lavender, and honeysuckles. There were several lakes and mountains in the background, which prompted me to remember how much my grandma loved her home in the mountains surrounded by a lake. Me, my parents, and younger brother spent a lot of time fishing out of the lake at grandma's house. Standing in the middle of a meadow were several people waving at us. The only person I recognized was my maternal grandpa, Larry, who had been dead for about five years. He was 91 years old when he died; now he looked to be about 35, and healthy.

My grandma stopped abruptly and told me that I had to go back. It wasn't my time and I couldn't stay. She said that she just wanted me to see how beautiful heaven is and that she was going to be in a wonderful place with my grandpa. I felt heartbroken—I wanted to stay in this beautiful place with my grandma and grandpa. She said that I would join her again one day after I had lived a long, wonderful life. She said the cancer I had was now gone and it would never return because I had much work left to do on earth. I woke up with tears streaming down my face. Although it was only seven o'clock in the morning, I immediately called my mom and told her about my dream. After I filled her in on the details, she could barely hold back the tears. She paused for a moment, took a deep breath, and before breaking down in tears, she said that grandma Betsy had died at the nursing home around six o'clock that morning. It was then that I realized what I had experienced wasn't just a dream, I had actually walked with grandma Betsy to the entrance of heaven.

To say that I was completely blown away by her dream

would be an understatement. I knew without a shadow of a doubt that what she had shared with me was real—she had actually walked with her grandma to the door of heaven and witnessed its splendor. I assessed her chest and right arm for swelling. Her right upper arm was the same girth as her left upper arm. There was absolutely no swelling in her right upper arm now. After assessing her, I told her I didn't see any swelling, and promised that as soon I got back to the nurses' station, I would call the doctor and let him know the swelling had resolved. I also told her I would ask the doctor to discharge her, but I couldn't promise he would.

Just as I promised, when I got back to the nurses' station, I called the doctor and told him about my findings. I explained the patient's grandmother had just died and she felt she needed to be with the family. I asked the doctor to please consider discharging her as soon as possible that day. He told me he was making rounds in the hospital and he would come right away to see her and write her discharge orders. Within two hours, my patient was on her way home. One week later, we received a nice card from Sarah, thanking the staff for the wonderful care she received and thanking me specifically for the compassion and loving care I gave her. God bless you Sarah! I will never forget you or your dream!

Near Death Experiences

Although near death experiences (NDEs) are becoming increasingly common—largely because of resuscitation and advanced life support techniques—there is no agreed upon, uniform definition of what a near death experience actually is. Nevertheless, I think Wikipedia offers a good working definition:

> A profound personal experience associated with death or impending death which researchers claim share similar characteristics. When positive, such experiences may encompass a variety of sensations including detachment from the body, feelings of levitation, total serenity, security, warmth, the experience of absolute dissolution, and the presence of a light. When negative, such experiences may include sensations of anguish and distress.

But what exactly are NDEs? Are they hallucinations? Spiritual experiences? Proof of life after death? Or are they simply chemical changes in the brain and sensory organs in the moments prior to death? These are the questions that prevent researchers and clinicians in the medical field from forming a more specific definition everyone can agree upon. Even though no consensus exists on the cause of NDEs, there are common traits of an NDE that most people experience. In Dr. Jeffrey Long's book, *Evidence of the Afterlife,* he states that no two near-death experiences are identical, but that a pattern of elements are usually seen and occur in a consistent order. He lists twelve elements identified from over 1,300 NDE cases he researched. He concluded that NDEs may include some or all of the these elements:

1. An out of body experience (OBE), which is separation of consciousness from the physical body.
2. Heightened senses—perceptions are more vivid.
3. Intense and generally positive emotions or feelings (not all NDEs are positive emotional experiences).
4. Passing into or through a tunnel.
5. Encountering a mystical or brilliant light.
6. Encountering other beings, either mystical beings, or deceased friends or relatives.
7. A sense of alteration of time or space.
8. Life review.
9. Encountering otherworldly realms.
10. Encountering or learning special knowledge.
11. Encountering a boundary or barrier.
12. A return to the body, either voluntary or involuntary.

In this section, I will recount the NDE's my patients shared with me. Many of these NDEs happened to patients whom I helped to resuscitate in the ICU. We ran our own codes and I was always assigned to a code team. So, I know for a fact that the patients I coded and who shared their NDE with me were clinically dead, not just swooning or unresponsive. Every patient who described their NDE to me had a different experience—some good, some bad. Regardless of the differences, their NDE contained many of the same elements as listed above.

Dale Goes to Hell and Comes Back to Tell About It!

Dale was a forty-seven year old male patient of mine on the cardiac step-down unit of a large urban hospital. He had suffered a massive heart attack at work and was rushed to our Emergency Department where he died and was resuscitated. After his cardiac angiogram, he was admitted to my floor so that we could monitor and prep him to have bypass surgery the next morning. His angiogram showed that the Left Anterior Descending (LAD) coronary artery was 100% occluded and the (RCA) Right Coronary Artery was 95% occluded. Early the next morning while I was doing some pre and post-surgical teaching to prepare him for what to expect, he told me a story that I will never forget. He said that when he died in the emergency room, he went to hell, but was rescued by Jesus. This is what he shared with me:

> I had just gotten to work at a new construction site close by the hospital when I experienced the worst crushing chest pain that you could imagine. The pain felt like I had a ten ton elephant standing on my chest. I remember not being able to breath before everything went black. After that, I felt myself being pulled up and out of my body. Then I had the sensation of being sucked backwards through a long dark tunnel. I could perceive other beings in the tunnel with me. They all seemed to be reaching out trying to grab me, but I was able to evade their grasp. I continued through this tunnel for a while longer before being dumped into what seemed like a deep, dark pit. I was surrounded by a dark gray fog, which I could see through at times. What I

saw through the breaks in the fog horrified me far more than any horror flick I've ever seen. There were several different creatures—part man and part animal. A few of these creatures had the head and snout of a pig and body of a man. Some had the head and hooves of a bull and the body of a man. Most had the head and beak of a turkey vulture and talons that were at least twelve inches long. All the these creatures produced a deep sense of fear and trembling within me, but the bird creatures with the long talons scare me most of all.

Once the creatures realized I was there, they started to attack me. The bull creatures trampled me with their hooves and impaled me with the horns. The pig creatures chewed on my flesh while the bird creatures ripped the flesh off my bones. I was so terrified that I couldn't stand it. It was then that I cried out for Jesus to save me. No sooner than the plea escaped from my lips, I saw a tiny blue orb off in the distance that started moving towards me. It became larger and larger as it moved closer to me, and I could feel an intense unconditional love emanating from it. Finally, this blue orb became big enough for me to see that there was a man standing in the center of it who was dressed in a white robe with a golden sash around his waist. It quickly occurred to me that this man was Jesus. All of a sudden I felt myself being jolted back into my body, and my eyes immediately popped open.

The first person I saw was the E.R. doctor bending over me. I begged him to keep me alive because I wasn't ready to die again—I didn't want to go back to hell. The doctor stopped what he was doing, glanced at me with a look of bewilderment on his face and said for me not to worry, he would do everything in his power to keep me alive. I asked the nurse if I could see my wife and within just a few minutes she was standing at my bedside. I told my wife to find a minister that would visit me in the hospital. With a worried look on her face, she asked me why. I told her that I had just seen the afterlife and I was a changed man. I didn't tell her about the horrors of hell that I had just experienced. I figured I would tell her later, after I knew for sure that I would survive this heart attack and live long enough to get right with God. My wife wasted no time in contacting a minister.

By the time I was finished with my heart catheterization, an episcopal minister was waiting for me in my room on the step-down unit. Once I finally made it to my room, I really just wanted to go to sleep. I was totally exhausted from everything I had been through and still groggy from the sedative they gave me in the cath lab. Nevertheless, I was relieved and elated to see the minister and wasted no time telling him about my experience in hell. I told him that I was ready and willing to do whatever I needed to do to be saved so that I never had to go back to there. I told him that I had been raised in a Baptist church, but stopped attending when I turned eighteen and moved out of my parents' house. The minister told me that the only thing I had to do to be saved is to believe that I am already saved by grace—that it's only by grace, not by works that we are saved. As he spoke these words to me, I could feel the unconditional love that I felt when I was rescued from hell by Jesus.

Dale's bypass surgery was uneventful, and he was admitted back to our unit after the customary three day stay in the CCU (Coronary Care Unit). I was working on the day he was readmitted and was assigned as his nurse. I asked him how everything went with the surgery. He said he apparently didn't die on the table, but if he had, he knew without a shadow of a doubt that he would have gone to heaven. He also told me he was no longer afraid of dying because Jesus had already saved him from hell and he wouldn't be going back. Instead, next time he died, he would be going to be with Jesus and his loved ones in heaven.

Hannah Goes to Heaven and Comes Back a Healer

Hannah was a 43 year old patient of mine on the ob/ gyn unit of a small rural hospital where I worked at the time. She was admitted for surgery—a hysterectomy—because of uterine hemorrhage secondary to endometriosis, which she had tolerated for many years until it became life threatening. I was Hannah's nurse on the day before she was scheduled to have surgery. While I was doing her pre and post-op teaching, she made the comment to me that she hoped things would go better for her this time because she died the last time she was in the hospital, which occurred when she delivered her twins sixteen years earlier. She said she had been hospitalized due to preeclampsia when she was eight months pregnant and her blood pressures were so high that the doctor thought she would have a stroke if he didn't induce labor soon.

She said soon after the doctor induced labor, she delivered the first twin. While she was giving birth to the second twin, her blood pressure skyrocketed and she died from a stroke. I stopped my teaching efforts and asked her if she would like to talk more about her death experience. She said she would love a chance to talk about it because she hadn't had many opportunities to do so. Her husband and mother were the only two people she had confided in about her experience. Her mother believed her, but her husband blew it off saying that it was more than likely just a hallucination. This was what she said happened to her when she died:

I was in the delivery room and had just delivered my second twin when I heard what I thought was the heart monitor alarm go off, and then I heard the nurse yell out, we've lost her! The next thing I knew, I was standing next to my bed, looking down on my body. I felt sorry for the condition of my body and wanted someone to help it. Chaos ensued and I watched as the doctor and nurses scurried about with the crash cart trying to resuscitate me. Suddenly, I was pulled head first through a tunnel full of bluish-white light. I perceived that there were other beings in the tunnel with me, but I couldn't see them because I was traveling so fast. Once I reached the end of the tunnel, I found myself standing in a beautiful garden filled with fruit bearing trees in various stages of bloom and fragrant, colorful flowers. In the background was a row of snow capped mountains nestled behind a huge sea and sandy, white beach. The crystal clear water of the sea sparkled in the sunlight as the surf met the shoreline. The sound of waves crashing on the shore sounded like celestial music to my ears. I had a sense of complete well being—I felt happy, whole, and deeply loved. As I looked closer at the sparkling sea, I saw Jesus walking on the water and coming towards me. He said it was up to me whether to come back to earth or not.

All of a sudden I remembered my husband and twin girls. I became overwhelming concerned about what would happen to them without me. My husband and girls needed me and I had to be there for them. I told Jesus I wanted to go back and be with my family. He told me I would suffer pain and disability at first, but that my physical body would heal completely and I would become a healing channel for others.

Almost immediately, I was thrust back into my body and could hear the doctor say, "We got her back; let's deliver the placenta and get her transferred to the ICU." My head felt as if it had been hit with a sledge hammer. For some reason, I couldn't open my eyes, but I could feel the doctor tugging on my insides, and with an almost unbearable cramp, I could feel the placenta being pulled out of me. I seemed to go in and out of consciousness, but I knew I was alive and my soul was present with my body. I perceived that something was physically wrong with me because I couldn't see or move. Then I remembered Jesus telling me I would suffer pain and disability at first, but then I would heal completely. I was happy to be alive with the hope of living a full, happy, and healthy life with my twin girls and husband.

My hospital course was almost miraculous given my prognosis—the doctor believed that I wouldn't be able to use my left arm, walk, or eat normally again. The stroke had affected my left side, especially my arm, which I couldn't move at all. I had some paralysis in my left leg, but I was still able to wiggle my toes and flex my foot. I didn't have a swallow reflex so I couldn't eat, and had to have a tube put in my nose so I could receive liquid nourishment. I was able to talk, but my words were confused and jumbled up sometimes.

After working with a physical therapist three times a week for three months, I made a full and miraculous recovery and was able to assume my role as a wife and mother. Since my near death experience, I have become more compassionate and considerate of people's feelings, beliefs, and needs. I am also more confident in God's love, and no longer afraid of death. I enjoy channeling God's healing power and have learned many different alternative healing modalities that I have incorporated in my practice as a healer. I am grateful for the second chance I've been given. I hope to be around for a long time to enjoy the love and life I have with my husband and children.

Hannah's surgery went well and she was discharged to home three days later, accompanied by her husband and twin girls. One week after her discharge, our unit received a card from Hannah thanking me and the rest of the staff for the compassionate and professional care we gave her. She also treated the day and night shift staff with enough pizza to feed an army.

Linda Refused to Enter the Light

I was Linda's nurse on the day shift for most of her stay in the intensive care unit. Linda was a 72 year old who was admitted through the emergency department (E.D.) with acute respiratory distress secondary to emphysema.

The E.D. doctor intubated her and placed her on a ventilator (vent) as soon as she arrived to the E.D. by ambulance. She stayed on the vent for seven days before we were able to start weaning her off. During the weaning process, she was fitted with a Passy Muir Valve over her tracheostomy tube so that she could talk. She wasn't able to speak when she was hooked up to the vent and she was so weak and shaky that she couldn't write legibly.

As soon as she had the opportunity to talk, she told me that she absolutely did not want to be resuscitated if she died. I was on my way out the door to her room when she made a comment that caught my attention and drew me back in. She said she wasn't afraid to die because she had died a long time ago, but chose not to go into the light. She said that in 1972 she had an emergency appendectomy because her appendix ruptured spewing bacteria into her abdomen. She quickly became septic from the infection (Sepsis is a dangerous infection in the blood stream that has spread throughout the body causing organ failure and ultimately death if not treated quickly). She told me that she died on the operating table during surgery. This was what Linda experienced:

> I was floating over my body, and I could see and hear everything that was being said and done. I watched as the surgeon pulled my intestines out of my abdomen and put them up and over to the side. I left the operating room for awhile and went out into the surgical waiting room where my parents and husband were sitting. I tried to talk to them and tell them I was okay,

but they couldn't hear or see me. So, I returned to the operating room and stood beside the table where my body lay. The nurses were running chaotically about the room, and I heard the doctor who was sitting by my head say, "Get the crash cart now!" I watched as this doctor injected some kind of drug into my intravenous line. I felt the sensation of warmth on my back and turned around to see where it was coming from. That's when I saw and intense bluish-white light that beckoned for me to come to it. I seemed to have no control over my spirit body and started floating involuntarily towards this light. As I got closer, I realized that within the light was a tunnel. Many people were in this tunnel, but I didn't know any of them. They were waving at me and telling me that I could join them. The unconditional love I felt coming from the tunnel made me want to enter in, but the whole situation just didn't seem right to me.

I turned away from the tunnel and floated back over to my body. I watched as the surgeon placed paddles on my chest and pressed the buttons. My whole body lifted at least five inches off of the operating table, and I felt like I had been slammed back into my body. I remembered hearing the surgeon say, "We got her back!"

I woke up in the recovery room and the doctor said that the surgery was a success. He didn't mention the fact that I had died on the table. About ten minutes after I woke up, they moved me to my hospital room. My parents and husband were waiting for me when I got there. As soon as the nurses got me settled in my bed and left the room, my mother sat down beside me and took my hand. With tears streaming down her face, she said that she was so thankful to God I was alive and was going to be okay. I asked her why she thought I wouldn't be alive. My question obviously caught her off guard because all of the color drained from her face and she became quiet. After a brief silence, she told me that while they were still operating on me, one of the nurses came out and told them that they had lost me, but they had gotten me back again and the surgery was going well. I thought to myself that what I experienced wasn't just a dream. I had actually died and my mother just confirmed it. I told her I knew I had died because I could see and hear everything that was going on. I told her about my experience—how I ventured outside my physical body and visited her, my dad and husband in the waiting room, but they couldn't see or hear me. I also told her about the light and the people in the tunnel who wanted me to go with them.

Soon after my near death experience, I researched other people's near death experiences and came to the realization there were other dimensions we could experience life in after physical death. I wasn't a spiritual person when I died on the table, and I had never given much thought up until that time about what happens when you die. Although I understand now, it was difficult for me to understand back then how a dimension other than the physical dimension could exist. How was it possible for me to see and hear everything that was going on in the operating room? How could I perceive having a body, other than my physical body that could travel from one place to another just by thinking about it?

After I died and came back, I started to notice that I had knowledge about things I shouldn't have known about. I also dreamed of events happening before they actually happened. For example, I had prophetic dreams about the upcoming deaths of several of my extended family members. My psychic abilities skyrocketed to the point where I was able to hang out my psychic shingle. I gave professional readings for over thirty years until I became disabled with emphysema.

Linda was completely weaned off her vent and transferred to the medical unit for observation for a few days before being discharged to home. She promised she would definitely quit smoking, but I perceived it would be too difficult for her to do so—she would light up as soon as she could get away from the hospital. Nevertheless, I maintained the hope that she would quit smoking, if for no other reason than to ease her breathing and keep herself out of the hospital and off the vent. She didn't live in the physical world too much longer after that. I know because she visited me at home about six months after I took care of her in the hospital. She said she just wanted to thank me for caring for her and to let me know that she was happy in her new (after) life.

Deathbed Visions

Deathbed visions, or DBVs, have been know to occur hours, days, or even weeks prior to death in the dying individual. Many biologically based theories that attempt to explain the cause of these visions abound, but not one of them can actually disprove the spiritual element that is experienced. Regardless of the cause, I have had many dying patients report having these visions and, in most cases, their experience was very comforting.

I noticed that DBVs could occur while my patients were asleep or wide awake. Sometimes they received information during their DBV regarding the situation of a living relative for which they had no prior knowledge because the information was being withheld by other living family members. Many of my patients who experienced DBVs reported seeing beautiful vistas, such as gardens, mountains, and the seashore. Most, however, reported having visions of a welcoming committee consisting of either friends, relatives, and/or religious figures who told them that they had come to escort them to heaven. Everyone of my patients who reported seeing a welcoming committee seemed to have a sense of peace and happiness at the prospect of being reunited with their loved ones. I don't believe my patients were delusional or hallucinating because the majority of them were completely aware of people and situations in the physical environment. They were just able to perceive another reality in addition to their physical reality. In this section, I will discuss some of the DBVs I have witnessed, especially in my palliative patients, as well as those that were reported to me by patients, friends, or family members.

Mr. Walker Sees the Walking Dead

I had Mr. Walker as a patient on the medical-surgical unit of a small community hospital where I worked part-time. He had been in and out of the hospital several times within a six month period battling prostate cancer. During this particular stay, he was admitted to the hospital because he was no longer able to catheterize himself due to a total obstruction in his urethra caused by a tumor. Even though he had a prostatectomy six months earlier, along with a course of chemotherapy and radiation, the cancer apparently was not caught soon enough and had already metastasized to the surrounding tissue as well as to his bones, liver, and lungs. Now, he didn't have much longer to live.

During this hospitalization he had urostomy surgery to create a stoma so that a tube could be placed to drain urine from his bladder because it was impossible to catheterize him. He was in much pain but refused to take anything more than Toradol or Motrin to treat his pain. After discussing his prognosis with the oncologist, Mr. Walker decided to become a palliative care patient. He also decided to have the doctor change his code status from a full code to a DNR (Do Not Resuscitate).

From the time of his dismal prognosis until his death about a week later, Mr. Walker remained coherent and aware of of his physical surroundings. His two sons, Robert and Ryan, took turns staying with him day and night. Both of them reported to me that their dad said he saw people walking around the room as well as out in the hallway. Of course, these people weren't physically present because the sons couldn't see them. When the sons asked him who the people were, he said some of them were fellow soldiers who died in WWII, but there were other people that he didn't know at all. The sons said that while he was having these visions, he was fully aware of the physical presence of visitors and was able to carry on intelligent and grounded conversations with them. It was as if he was experiencing two worlds at once without compromising the reality of either one.

On the day he died, his sons told me that at about 11 pm the night before, when all was quiet, their dad looked over at the door and said, "Oh my darling! Come in! I've been missing you for such a long time!" When the sons asked their father to whom he was speaking, he replied, "Your beautiful mother. She has come to get me. She says that we'll be leaving soon. My father, mother, and brother are also here. They're saying they are here to take me home." During the early morning hours, their father was in and out of a fretful sleep in which he was having audible conversations with his dead visitors. The night nurse and nursing assistant witnessed these conversations and told me about them that morning during report. Tonya, the night nurse said that I had better be prepared for Mr. Walker to die that day because his folks were here to take him away.

Sure enough, Tonya was right in her assumption. Mr. Walker died peacefully later that afternoon surrounded by friends and family. His sons had big band music playing in the background. The oldest son, Robert, said that when they were small children, their parents would dance around the house with each other while listening to big band music. I was present at the bedside when Mr. Walker took his last breath. He had a big smile along with the most pleasing expression on his face that I had ever seen in someone who had just died. I asked Spirit to let me see Mr. Walker's spirit. I was granted my request and watched as he danced his beautiful wife up the steps of a golden staircase and onto silvery-white fluffy clouds. They were surrounded by family and friends on the other side who were clapping and cheering them on. I heard Mr. Walker say "Thank you for all you did for me. I am so happy to be reunited with my beautiful wife." Then the vision faded and I became aware of the tears streaming down my face. There wasn't a dry eye in the room; everyone had tears streaming down their faces as they said their goodbyes to this greatly loved man.

Mrs. Rivera Takes a Gondola Ride on the Grand Canal of Death

Mrs. Rivera was a 92 year old patient of mine on the cardiac step-down unit of a large trauma center. She was admitted through the emergency department after suffering a massive heart attack. She had a history of severe cardiomyopathy and was frequently in and out of the hospital with congestive heart failure. Cardiomyopathy is an enlargement of the heart muscle not caused by problems with the coronary arteries or blood flow. The damage that occurs to the heart in cardiomyopathy can be caused by viruses, alcohol, drug abuse, smoking, genetics, or pregnancy. Therefore, the placement of stents or bypass surgery would not have helped her.

The heart is a pump and cardiomyopathy causes the pump to fail. She would need a new heart in order to live.

The doctor told the family her heart failure was so bad there was nothing else they could do. She had an ejection fraction less than 5% and might not make it through the night. The left ventricle pumps only a fraction of the blood it contains. A normal ejection fraction is more than 55% of the blood volume. When the heart becomes enlarged, even if the amount of blood being pumped by the left ventricle remains the same, the relative fraction of blood being ejected decreases.

Because of her grim prognosis, Mrs. Rivera's family gathered around her bed holding vigil and saying prayers. Most of the nursing staff knew Mrs. Rivera because she had been a patient on our unit so often. The nursing staff absolutely loved and adored her. She was a sweet, kind, and giving lady who was always more concerned for our wellbeing than for her own. She always made sure her family took care of us. On previous admissions, we frequently overheard her talking to her children over the phone, instructing them to bring us pizza, bagels, or some delicious homemade Italian dish or confection. She kept a large bowl filled with candy and another large bowl filled with fruit in her room so that she could feed us. Whenever we entered her room, she would always say, "Mangia! Mangia!" (an Italian word that is a command to eat). So, Mrs. Rivera was always commanding us to eat! Mrs. Rivera came to this country from Venice, Italy with her husband before the start of WWII. Together, while raising a large family, they started a chain of very successful Italian restaurants. I believe that feeding people was one of the many ways she showed them love.

Mrs. Rivera made it through the night. The night nurse told me during report that she slept well, her vital signs were stable and her respirations were even and unlabored on high flow oxygen. The extended family held vigil in the waiting room while her seven children took turns staying at the bedside. When I walked into her room immediately after getting report, one of her daughters who was there told me her mother had slept peacefully throughout the night. While I was assessing her, she opened her eyes and looked up at me with a pleasant smile on her face. She said that she had had a dream and was no longer afraid of death. The sense of peace and joy she projected was overwhelming and contagious. I could tell she was beaming at the chance to tell her dream, so I stopped my assessment, held her hand, and asked her if she wanted to talk about her dream. She squeezed my hand and said in her Italian accent that she thought I would never ask. This was what she dreamed:

> I dreamed I was in a gondola on the grand canal of death. There were people in other gondolas going in the same direction as me. I could see a shoreline on the horizon. I just wanted to get to there so I could rest on the beach. The sand glittered like a hundred thousand diamonds reflecting the brightest sunshine I have ever seen. I looked up at the sun and it didn't hurt my eyes. The warm rays it emanated bathed my whole body in light, and I felt so whole and good. The blessed Madonna was kneeling at the shoreline, and I knew she was praying for me. Everyone was there, waiting for me to arrive—me sposa and amore Giuseppe, mama, papa,

me fratello Joseph, Zio Michael and Zia Nora. While I was thinking about how much I wanted to hurry and get to the shore, I saw Jesus walking on the water towards me. He reached out with his arms, lifted me out of the gondola and put me back in my bed. He told me to wait one more day and he would take me home. The holy angels sang glorious songs to me all night long.

I had Mrs Rivera as a patient the next day and she was in no obvious distress. She was alert and oriented to herself, place, and time. She was pleasant and offered no complaints. I didn't see any signs that she was dying—there was no mottling of the skin, her respirations were even and unlabored, and her urine output was adequate. Regardless of the absence of the signs of impending death, she passed away during the night, about four o'clock the next morning. The night nurse told me in report that morning that Mrs. Rivera had a big smile and radiant glow on her face when she died. My mind went back to her description of the sunshine. I'm sure the glow on her face was the result of the sunbeams of heaven shining down upon her.

Mr. Holloway's Deathbed Visions of Hell

Mr. Holloway was a patient of mine on the Intensive Care Unit. He was terminally ill with severe heart failure and was unable to perform even the most simple tasks without experiencing angina and shortness of breath. He was definitely in the end stage of his disease and not expected to live much longer. Mr. Holloway was not the nicest of patients. He was very sarcastic, demeaning, unrealistically demanding, and manipulative towards the whole nursing staff. He constantly screamed at us and was always trying to throw us out of his room, but yet he wanted to stay in the ICU. We weren't the only ones he took his frustrations out on—he literally put his wife through a living hell.

I walked into Mr. Holloway's room early one morning to do his assessment. As soon as I crossed the threshold of the door, he became extremely upset and yelled at me while pointing at the ceiling, "They came to get me last night and I told them to go away. Now they're back!" He looked up towards the far corner of the ceiling, waved his hand and said to his invisible visitors, "Go away! I'm not ready!" He looked at me with horror in his eyes and told me to tell them to go away and not come back! I looked towards the corner of the room where he had fixed his gaze and told his invisible visitors to go away and not come back. I completed my assessment of him and started out the door when he screamed, "Where's my wife? Call and get her in here now!" I reassured him that I would call his wife. As I walked out of his room, he started swatting at his invisible visitors while yelling at them to go away.

I called his wife a few minutes later to give her an update on Mr. Holloway's behavior, and to let her know he wanted her to come to the hospital. She said she was on her way and would arrive soon. I stuck my head into the door of his room and told him that everything would be okay—his wife was on the way to the hospital. He mumbled something, but I couldn't understand what he was saying. He didn't acknowledge my presence at all; instead, he just stared at the far corner of his room. Fifteen minutes later, his wife arrived and sat by his side. He didn't acknowledge her presence either. He just lay there in some kind of trance state with a look of horror on his face.

Mr. Holloway remained in a trance-like state until he passed away later that afternoon around four o'clock. While in this trance state, he constantly carried on a conversation with someone not physically present. He would also frequently strike out with his arms as if he were fending off an invisible attacker. As the day progressed, the signs of his impending death became more apparent. His skin became mottled, he stopped producing urine, and started exhibiting Cheyne-Stokes respirations (Cheyne-Stokes respirations is an abnormal pattern of breathing commonly seen as patients approach death). His heart rate increased as his blood pressure decreased. Just before he drew his last breath, his eyes flew wide open, and he clearly exclaimed, "Mama, I've been praying that you would come and take me to heaven!" No sooner than he had gotten these words out, he closed his eyes and died.

I looked up at the corner of the ceiling where Mr. Holloway had often gazed and saw a bluish-white mist. I immediately had a vision of a beautiful young woman with long black hair wearing a light blue chiffon dress. She had taken Mr. Holloway by the hand and was leading him up a sparkling silver-white staircase. They continued ascending the staircase until they disappeared above white fluffy clouds. My attention returned to the room and the presence of Mrs. Holloway who had tears streaming down her face. She stood up, bent over and kissed him on the forehead before quickly disappearing out the door. I looked down at Mr. Holloway and was pleased to see that the expression of torment he had for so long was now replaced with an expression of peace. He also seemed to be smiling. At that moment I knew, without a shadow of a doubt, that God had rescued him from his hellish existence and taken him to heaven.

I had prayed for the soul of Mr. Holloway all afternoon until the time of his death. I asked God to be gracious and rescue him from his torment. I maintained full faith that God had heard and would honor my request, and I believed it would definitely be done. I was so happy my prayers had been answered and he was no longer a tormented soul. Although he put many people through hell during his hospital stay with us, I was relieved to know that he didn't have to experience any more hell.

~ Eight ~

TRAPPED EARTHBOUND
SPIRITS

"Yet, despite all, it is a difficult thing to admit the existence of ghosts in a coldly factual world. One's very in-
stincts rebel at the admission of such maddening
possibility. For, once the initial step is made into the supernatural, there is no turning back, no knowing where
the strange road leads except that it is quite unknown
and quite terrible."

—Richard Matheson

Where's my Baby?

I was not hired to work the night shift at this small, rural
hospital, which I'll refer to as the Jay County General;
however, because of the nursing shortage we were experiencing for the night shift, all the nurses on the Orthopedic
and Mother Baby units were required to rotate days and
nights every two weeks. I was assigned to alternate between these two units on each six-week schedule while ro-

tating shifts. Working the night shift definitely did not agree with my own circadian rhythm. I never liked working nights because it was such a struggle for me. I had a very hard time sleeping during the day, even with blackout curtains in my bedroom. If the sun was up, my body automatically knew it and would say to me, "Get up! The sun is shining outside. You're supposed to be awake." At night, the cessation of the hustle and bustle of daily activities created by diagnostic and surgical services faded into a deathly silence that permeated every nook and cranny of the nursing unit.

For a Psychic Medium, the dead calm that settles over a hospital nursing unit when the lights are dimmed and the patients are sleeping is very conducive to receiving spirit communication. Add to this the hotbed of spirit activity in an old hospital and you have the perfect combination for continual bombardment by spirit entities. Most of the entities that contact me at work are restless souls trying to resolve unfinished business. These souls are trapped in the astral plane and need help in crossing over. While working at this hospital, I encountered many of these "lost souls." One such soul was a woman named Maddie.

I met Maddie about two o'clock in the morning as I was walking down the Mother-Baby hall on the way to a patient's room. I was about half way down the hall when I saw the spirit of a young woman coming out of a patient's room about two doors down from me on the left hand side of the hall. As I looked a little closer, I noticed that she was floating in mid-air. She had her hands over her eyes and appeared to be sobbing. She was wearing an old-fashioned looking, white cotton hospital gown. At first sight, this ghost looked so solid I thought she was a living person. I asked her for her name—she stopped crying, looked up at me and said, "My name is Madeline but they call me Maddie. Somebody took my baby and I don't know where he is. Can you help me find him?"

As she was speaking, she moved closer and stopped about three feet in front of me. From this distance I could see that she had light brown hair, which was long and disheveled; her face was was oval; her nose was long and narrow; her lips were thin; and she had blue eyes. She looked to be about five feet tall and slender. I said that I was sorry, but I had not seen her baby. I told her that she needed to come with me to an empty room so that we could talk without being disturbed. She followed me into the next room on my left, which was empty. I asked her what she remembered about her baby. She replied, "The nurse took my baby away while I was in bed. I could hear him crying but I couldn't move or get out of bed to get to him and I haven't seen him since. I have looked everywhere and I can't find him." While listening to her story, it occurred to me that Maddie could have died from any number postpartum complications, such as the following:

- Hemorrhage.
- Puerperal Fever in the days before antibiotics was a common cause of postpartum mortality.
- Preeclampsia, which is a serious blood pressure

condition that can happen after the 20th week of pregnancy or after giving birth.

- Milk leg is a condition in which blood clots in the legs can travel to the heart or lungs resulting in death.

- Amniotic embolism occurs when the fluid surrounding the baby makes its way into the mother's blood circulation during or shortly after labor resulting in the death of the mother. Even now, an amniotic embolism is considered a leading cause of maternal mortality in childbirth.

I asked Maddie if she could remember what was happening to her before they took her baby away.

She said, "I think I felt light-headed, and they said there was a lot of blood everywhere. I remember them rubbing my belly and it started to hurt really bad. That's all I remember. What did they do with my baby?"

I replied, "Maddie, I think they had to hold your baby for you because you needed help with your womb, which is the part of your body that contained and nurtured your baby while he was inside of you. After the doctor delivered your baby, your womb was soft and boggy and failed to contract enough to slow down the bleeding. That's why they rubbed your belly hoping that it would cause your womb to firm up and slow down the blood flow. Maddie, it sounds as if you may have passed away because you lost too much blood."

She said, "What are you talking about? If I were dead, I

would be in heaven with Jesus. I wouldn't be here looking for my baby!"

I replied, "Your need to find your baby in the earth realm is probably keeping you from crossing over into heaven. You can reunite with your baby when you cross over into the light, where you will also be with other loved ones, Jesus and God."

She looked puzzled for a moment and asked, "Am I really dead?"

I told her, "Yes, honey, you have passed out of your physical body and are in your astral body. You can go be with Jesus in the light and be reunited with your baby who may be all grown up by now, but he is still your baby."

I created a portal by visualizing an arched doorway with the light of Heaven shining through and told her that she could walk through it and be reunited with her baby and other loved ones that had already crossed over. She stepped one foot over the threshold of the portal and turned around to look at me. I looked at her reassuringly and told her that it was okay, she could go on.

She said, "I see my baby; he's all grown up, and he's with my mother, father, and my grandchildren. Thank you! I will see you again one day and introduce you to my family!" Maddie disappeared from my sight and the portal closed.

Where's my Wife?

Not long after I started my new job as Clinical Quality Director at E. H. Hospital I encountered the Sundowner. I was walking towards the rear entrance of the hospital late one winter afternoon as the sun was setting and casting its warm, orange glow on the floor and walls of the corridor, when I encountered the spirit of a short, thin elderly man dressed in a light blue hospital gown. He floated in front of me once from my left to my right and then started to pace along my left side as I continued to walk.

He started shouting, "Help! Help! Help!"

When I asked him why he was shouting, "Help," he replied, "I don't know where my wife is. The nurses won't let me go home. They say I'm confused and I have to stay here. They even tie me down at night."

As I stopped and looked around, I realized that the locked door to my left led to the psychiatric unit. This was the only door that connected the psychiatric unit to the rest of the hospital. While standing there, it occurred to me that this spirit had been a psychiatric patient on the unit when he passed away and never understood that he had died. His belief that he was physically restrained by the hospital nursing staff kept him from seeing the light and crossing over.

I asked this spirit if he knew he had passed away, that he no longer had a physical body.

He replied, "What are you talking about?"

I told him he no longer had a physical body and that he could go to heaven if he wanted to.

He stopped pacing, looked straight at me and said, "Lady, you're the one who's crazy. I have a body. I can see my body. I know I have a body. I'm not that crazy."

I thought to myself: *Well, I was right about him coming from the psychiatric unit.*

He went on to say, "Look, Lady, I just want to go home to my wife. Can you help me do that?"

I asked him if he saw a light or tunnel with light at the end of it.

He replied, "No."

I told him that if he listened to me and did exactly as I said, I could help him go home.

He happily agreed and said, "Okay, but please hurry up!"

In my mind, I created an opening to a heavenly paradise at the far end of the hallway. I called upon Holy Angels and loved ones in Spirit to come and greet this lost soul at the entrance to the light and to escort him to the level of heaven where paradise exists. I also asked them to reconnect him with his wife at some point in time.

I then told this lost soul that for him to be discharged and sent home where he could be with his wife, he would have to come with me to the big light at the end of the hall so that the discharge attendants could take him home.

He said, "Okay, let's go!"

I turned and walked back down the hall in the opposite direction from where I was originally headed. I asked him if he could see the attendants standing just inside the bright light.

He said, "Yes. How come they have so many lights on?"

I told him they had a lot of lights on because they need to be able to see which way to go to take people home from the hospital. When we reached the end of the hall, I said good-bye and watched as this rescued soul stepped into the entrance of the Light and was quickly carried away by angels and his loved ones in Spirit. He never looked back. I watched as the Light got smaller and smaller and was no longer visible. Once the light completely disappeared, I continued to walk through the front entrance of the hospital. I decided to go to my office, get my purse, and call it a day. I was feeling a little drained, I had definitely gone beyond the call of duty that day and was ready to go to my own home!

Nurse Nora is Trapped in Hospital Purgatory

In 1965, Nurse Nora worked on the medical-surgical unit of the county hospital, which a couple of decades later became the step-down coronary care unit. I first encountered Nurse Nora when I worked on this unit in the 1990's. I was in the medication room taking meds out of the Pyxis (a medication dispensing machine) for my last patient during the morning med pass when I started experiencing a glitch with the Pyxis. The drawer I needed to get NPH insulin from was stuck and would not open. I called the pharmacy and told them about the problem with the Pyxis. I turned around to exit through the med room door, and that's when I saw Nurse Nora.

She was beautiful with her olive complexion, brown eyes, and shoulder length black hair that curled up at the ends. She was wearing a starchy white dress uniform, white stockings, lace-up white shoes that had a one-inch heal, and a dutch style nurse's cap with one black stripe. She said to me in a low whisper, "Be careful. Don't kill your patient like I did." I was shaken to the core by her comment. What did she mean? Was this a warning or was I actually going to kill one of my patients? Of course, it wouldn't be intentional if I killed anyone. I began to wonder if she had anything to do with the Pyxis drawer malfunctioning. I asked her what she meant by her comment and if she caused the drawer to malfunction. She didn't answer me—she just faded away.

I walked out of the med room and went to my computer to do some charting until the drawer was recovered. I was still shaken by her comment and wondered why she wouldn't answer my questions. Fifteen minutes later a pharmacy tech appeared and told me that the problem with the drawer was resolved and that he was glad that I couldn't get the drawer open because I might have given the wrong insulin if I hadn't checked the bottle closely. There was regular, short acting insulin in the drawer when it should have be long acting NPH. He said that he removed the regular insulin and replaced it with NPH. I don't know who was to blame for putting the wrong type of insulin in the drawer, but I do know it could have been lethal for someone if they received a large dose of regular insulin instead of the NPH. We normally gave patients regular insulin per a sliding scale based on their blood sugar level, which is usually a much smaller dose than an NPH dose.

At that time we had the "Five Rights" of medication administration that we had to use before administering any drug. The "Five Rights" is a protocol followed by nurses to increase patient safety by decreasing drug errors. The five rights are: right drug, right dose, right route, right patient, right time. Insulin bottles tend to look alike at first glance, and any nurse who pulled the regular insulin in haste without checking closely to make sure it was the NPH could have easily killed their patient by administering a lethal dose of regular insulin. Ironically, the use of a Pyxis or similar medication dispensing machine is supposed to improve patient safety, but it definitely doesn't prevent medication dispensing errors. The only thing that can help prevent medication errors is a system of checks such as the five rights of medication administration. Anyway, a potential medication error had occurred and I needed to inform my charge nurse and submit an incident report.

I filled out an incident report with details about what the pharmacy tech had said about the regular insulin being in the NPH drawer and about the drawer malfunctioning. Of course, I didn't give any details in the report about my experience with the ghost nurse. Then, I walked up to the main nurse's station and told my charge nurse, Mrs. Folchetti, about the mix up of insulins in the Pyxis. Because I knew that Mrs. Folchetti was a believer, I also told her about my encounter with the ghost nurse who warned me not to kill my patient and apparently caused the NPH drawer to malfunction so that it wouldn't open. I gave Mrs. Folchetti a physical description of the ghost nurse I saw and she exclaimed, "Oh my god! You just described Nora, a nurse that I worked with on this floor when it was still a medical-surgical unit thirty years ago." She proceeded to tell me Nora's story:

One of Nora's patients who had below the knee amputation surgery two days earlier died after she gave him a dose of morphine. That night at home, she committed suicide by slitting her wrists. She was single and lived alone, so there was no one there to help prevent it. It was so tragic; she was twenty-five years old, very beautiful and had a promising future. All the doctors wanted to date her.

It was later discovered in the court proceedings that her patient's wife had given him Numorphan (an opioid pain killer popular during the 60's before it was banned) It is being used again under a different name), and Valium (a benzodiazepine sedative that came out in the early 1960's—commonly prescribed for anxiety), and Librium (also a benzodiazepine sedative that was popular and commonly prescribed in the 1960's for anxiety). After taking these drugs, he asked Nora for his IV morphine and she gave it, not knowing that his wife had already given him all of the other drugs. He actually died from a narcotic cocktail, not the morphine dose. Nora checked his respirations before giving him the injection and they were 16 a minute—within normal range for safely giving morphine. However, the morphine had a synergistic effect on the other drugs, which quickly depressed his respirations and lead to respiratory arrest.

His wife should not have been medicating him, but he asked her for the drugs she gave them. He had been taking anxiolytics and narcotics for several years to treat anxiety and chronic back pain related to an injury he received in WWII. According to the wife's court testimony, he was addicted to these drugs and demanded them. She said she had no idea that the medication could kill him. Nora did not know that his wife had given him drugs, otherwise she wouldn't have medicated him. She was an excellent and caring nurse; she did nothing wrong and didn't deserve to be a second victim. It's so sad that she took her own life thinking that she had caused someone else's death when she actually didn't.

I asked Mrs. Folchetti if she would join me in trying to cross Nora over. She gladly agreed and we made plans to meet at my house the next day since we were both scheduled to be off duty. She came over around eleven o'clock the next morning. We sat down at the kitchen table, joined hands and called out for Nora to join us. Nora showed up almost immediately—the room grew icy cold and I could see her standing behind Mrs. Folchetti's chair. At my request, Mrs. Folchetti told Nora the truth about what really happened. We both emphasized to her that it wasn't her fault the patient died. I told her that she shouldn't pay penance anymore for what happened because she was innocent. She was now free to go to heaven. In my mind, I created a doorway to heaven in the middle of the room and called on Nora's angels and loved ones to come and take her to heaven. The most beautiful angels surrounded by golden light showed up along with several nuns, a couple of nurses, and many loved ones to escort her to heaven. She said she would continue to watch over us as we cared for our patients and then she faded away along with her heavenly host. Tears are flowing down my face as I sit here writing. Since her crossing, I have often felt her protective presence as I cared for my own patients.

Gangster Ghosts on the Loose in the Hospital!

I was sitting at the desk in my foyer on the cardiac step-down unit trying to get some computer charting done when this gangster ghost ran up from behind me on my right side and hid under my desk. I asked him what he was doing and why he had a gun.

He responded, "Shush lady! I'm waiting for the crab (the most disrespectful slur Bloods use to refer to a member of the Crips) to come through here cause I'm a Blood and a CK (crip killer)."

I asked him what in the world he was talking about.

He said, "Lady be quiet or I'll shoot you!"

I laughed at him and asked him what he planned to use to shoot me.

He jumped out from under the desk, got in my face and said, "Bitch, I know you didn't say that! I'll kill you!"

I told him I didn't think that was going to happen because he was a ghost and his gun wasn't real.

"What the hell are you talking about bitch! You better know this gun is real! I killed a damn crip with it and I'll kill you too!"

No sooner than he had gotten those words out, a Crip gangster ghost appeared in front of my desk out of nowhere and started shooting his ghost gun. The Blood gangster who was just in my face turned around and returned fire. They both fell to the floor after apparently shooting each other fatally; then, they just disappeared. I shook my head and wondered why I had just witnessed this ghostly duel. Was I supposed to try and cross them over? If I did, I'm certain they would be headed for hell. Or, were they already in a type of hell or purgatory where they had to continually kill each other and experience dying for all eternity?

I ran downstairs to the cafeteria at lunchtime because I didn't make lunch for myself that day. I went through line and got my favorite lunch meal at the hospital, a tuna pita, potato chips, and a root beer. I noticed there were several Emergency Department nurses sitting at a table in the corner of the dining room. I walked over, introduced myself and asked if I could join them. During my conversation with the E.D. nurses, I asked them how often they treated gang members with gunshot wounds. Danny, the E.D. charge nurse, spoke up and said:

> We treat them more often than we would like to. They deserve treatment just like anyone else, but you can cut the tension in the E.D. with a knife when we're treating gang members. It's just that you don't know when a member of another gang might come through the door wielding a gun and shooting everyone in the process of taking out his rival. Not only that, but they can turn on you in a New York second and cause some real damage to the nurses and other patients. We had two rival members come through our doors just last week, one

was a Blood and the other was a Crip. They both ended up dying while we were working on them. We just knew that their gang members were going to show up in the E.D. and start a war with each other. Fortunately, that didn't happen because we stepped up our hospital security and got the city police involved as well.

Although it was tempting, I didn't mention the ghostly shoot-out I witnessed in my foyer that morning. I thought to myself that they would think either that I was a nut case or making the story up to get special attention. Anyway, I knew that the gangsters I saw were the same ones who died in the E.D. the week before. I also knew that they would be spending their eternities trapped in hospital purgatory.

~ Nine ~

GHOSTS ATTACHED TO MY
PATIENTS

"It's okay, if you don't want to believe in ghosts. It
doesn't change anything. They still believe in you."
—Jason Medina

Earthbound Ghosts

What happens after the death of the physical body is
crucial. Normally the soul goes to the Light and enters the spiritual planes, but not always. It can stay on the
earth plane, a misfortune for which there are many reasons. It may then attach to human beings or to a location.
Ghosts that attach their consciousness and energy to a living person are called possessing spirits. These earthbound
spirits need energy, and many places exist where they can
lurk when looking for someone to attach to or possess.
Many ghosts are found in places such as bars, jails, pris-
ons, and nursing homes; none of these places, however,
seems to be as infested with ghosts as hospitals. Anyone

spending time in a hospital is particularly vulnerable to attracting possessing spirits. Just sitting in a hospital waiting room can get you noticed by earthbound ghosts. In her book, *The Unquiet Dead: A Psychologists Treats Spirit Possession,* Dr. Edith Fiore writes the following about the amount of spirits hanging out in hospitals:

> If we could see clairvoyantly, we would probably be shocked at the number of spirits that populate hospitals. People die, often drugged or in a state of confusion and fear, and may remain there, earthbound. Most—not realizing they are dead—expect the nurses and doctors to continue taking care of them—sometimes to the extent of possessing them. One entered my patient, a male nurse, while he was administrating mouth-to-mouth resuscitation as the spirit's body died from a drug overdose. Other spirits are so desperate to live that they bulldoze their way into any victims who suit their purposes.

Most of the earthbound souls you would expect to find hanging out in a hospital are either ghosts who are trapped because they are lost and confused, or hungry ghosts who can't return to their own body so they look for a body through which they can live vicariously. It is easy to understand why the spirit of someone who died from trauma might become confused and wander around the ethereal corridors and rooms of a hospital for years on end. There are, however, many ghosts that die while in the hospital who made a conscious decision not to cross over. There are various reasons why ghosts choose not to cross over:

- They have a fear of judgment for negative deeds committed while in their physical body.
- They have unfinished business.
- They stay behind to protect a loved one.
- They are obsessed with a living person.
- They don't believe in life after death—they think that if they leave the earth plane, they will cease to exist..
- They seek someone to attach to or possess someone so that they can continue to enjoy the desires they experienced while in their physical body. These desires may include, but are not limited to sex, drugs, alcohol, food, sports and other activities.

Earthbound ghosts who seek someone to attach to or possess so that they can fulfill the "fleshy" desires of the physical body are sometimes referred to as hungry ghosts. They remember how they enjoyed eating, drinking, doing drugs, having sex, and other activities, so they attach themselves to the living in hopes of having the experiences they had when they were in their own body. People who were strongly addicted to or obsessed with certain desires while alive are the ones that usually become hungry ghosts when they die. Individuals with strong addictions have sometimes been described by therapists as people who have transformed into hungry ghosts while still alive. In her online article, *The Little-Known Buddhist Realm Of Hungry Ghosts,* Ginelle Testa describes what hungry ghost are and what they look like:

In Buddhist cosmology, there are six realms. The man-
dala, or the Buddhist wheel of life, goes through each of
them. One of them is the Realm of the Hungry Ghosts.
It's a description, really, of us in this state. It is supposed to reflect human characteristics. This realm just
happens to have beings depicted in it that are shown as
having narrow necks so that no food can pass through
and huge bellies to house all that desire. These creatures are really reflecting an endless desire for satisfac-
tion and inability to be satisfied. It is an exaggerated
version of human craving. Picture that gnawing sensation, when you're really desiring for something. It
makes your fists clench and that clenching sensation is
sent through your entire body. The desire is a desper-
ate feeling as if you'll lose it without having the object
of your affection. It could be alcohol, food, people, or
more. These are our attachments and addictions.

Hungry ghosts usually look for someone whose mind is
on the same wavelength as theirs because they are easy to
possess. Living people with addictions have a highly negative energy field and a ghost who has the same kind of energetic pattern will choose to live vicariously through the
living person who is dealing with those addiction. Drugs
and excessive alcohol intake not only diminish the body's
natural aura, but it is believed they actually cause rips
or gaps in this protective shield and in the psyche itself.
Earthbound ghosts, even those who are just lost and confused, can and will attach themselves to anyone who has
a weakened aura. Severe illness also greatly impairs the
aura, making most patients vulnerable to spirit attachment. Later on in this chapter, I will share with you two of
the most fascinating encounters I've had with earthbound

ghosts who were either trying to attach or had already attached to a patient. But first, I want to tell you how I perceive any kind of attachment, no matter what type—ghost or demon..

How I Perceive Attachments

I can perceive attachments just by looking at the color of someone's aura. When I see a black blob (sometimes it looks like an ink blot) usually near someone's head, abdomen or back, I'm one hundred percent sure they have an attachment. Most of the time, if I look closer, I can also see the form of the possessing spirit within the victim's body. My angel of protection, St. Michael, also tells me when someone has an attachment, as well as the kind of entity that is attached. It is almost impossible for attached or possessing entities to hide from my perception. Auras are also very helpful to me in analyzing someone's state of being. I assessed the auras of my patients during my nursing career as a way to confirm the psychic impressions I had about them and to complement their physical assessment. I did this in an effort to provide them with the most therapeutic care possible. Below, I have listed the colors commonly seen in an aura and what they typically represent:

- **Red:** Strong willed, sensual, passionate, competitive
- **Dark Red:** Angry, unforgiving personality

- **Orange:** Creative, sociable and courageous
- **Dark Orange**: Lazy, low level of ambition, repressed creative abilities
- **Yellow:** Inspiration and intelligence, Prone to continued thought or study, Writers and other creative individuals
- **Dark Yellow**: Occupied with stressful thoughts or constant worrying
- **Green:** Prosperity and growth
- **Dark Green**: Jealousy, insecurity, sensitive to criticism
- **Turquoise:** Rapid healing
- **Blue:** Calm, cool and collected
- **Light Blue:** Peaceful, intuitive
- **Royal Blue:** Very spiritual, clairvoyant, and generous
- **Muddy Blue**: Fear of speaking
- **Indigo:** Open third eye and clairvoyance, psychic abilities
- **Violet:** Intuition, insight, psychic power, magical, and artistic ability
- **Lavender:** Imagination, vision and daydreaming
- **Silver:** Abundance, money or a spiritual awakening
- **Gray:** Blocked energy, guarded, skepticism.
- **Gold:** Divine wisdom, protection, enlightenment, unconditional love
- **Black:** Grief, health problems, impending death
- **Black spot or ink blot:** An entity attachment

- **White:** Spirituality, truth, purity, angelic qualities, Source energy (God)
- **Rainbow:** Healing virtue
- **Brown:** Materialistic concerns, self absorption
- **Dark Brown:** Depression, illness

As you can see from looking at the descriptions above, the color of an aura can reveal a lot about someone's state of being. The great American mystic and sleeping prophet Edgar Cayce stated the following in his essay on auras:

An aura is an effect, not a cause. Every atom, every molecule, every group of atoms and molecules however, simple or complex, however large or small, tells the story of itself, its pattern, its purpose, through the vibrations which emanate from it. Colors are the perceptions of these vibrations by the human eye. As the souls of individuals travel through the realms of being they shift and change their patterns as they use or abuse the opportunities presented to them. Thus at any time, in any world, a soul will give off through vibrations the story of itself and the condition in which it now exists. If another consciousness can apprehend those vibrations and understand them it will know the state of its fellow being, the plight he is in, or the progress he has made.

The Ghost of an Overdosed Prostitute Attaches to Jenny

I admitted and took care of Jenny after her surgery on the ob/gyn unit of small rural hospital. Jenny was a twenty-eight year old wife and mother of four small children with an admission diagnosis of ovarian cancer. She was scheduled to have a total abdominal hysterectomy with a salpingo-oophorectomy the next day, which is an operation to remove the uterus, fallopian tubes, and ovaries. When I admitted Jenny, she had no attachments. Her aura was green, brown, and red. These are the colors of someone healing from an illness and who is also angry, possibly over their illness. There were no black spots that might be indicative of an attachment in her aura at all. However, that changed the next day.

She returned to her room from post-op with a very obvious attachment in her aura. Apparently she had picked up this attachment while she was unconscious from the anesthesia. The reason I speculate that the attachment occurred while she was unconscious is that anesthesia significantly weakens an already weakened aura. Any surgery, which involves anesthesia that alters one's consciousness also alters etheric protection. While under the influence of anesthesia the aura is open and susceptible to different forms of psychic attack and spiritual attachment. Ideally, psychic protection needs to be implemented before the administration of any kind of consciousness altering anesthesia if possible. At the end of this chapter, I will cover psychic protection techniques that can be used before going under the influence of consciousness altering anesthesia.

Jenny's ghost attachment was very obvious as it actually had a humanoid form. It had attached itself, but the connection was weak and not complete. The entity had submerged its body into Jenny's aura, but its head and shoulders was still in the astral realm. When Jenny returned to her room, she was still very lethargic from the effects of general anesthesia and not very responsive. I assessed her lower abdominal surgical wound dressing, feminine pad, and vital signs before addressing her attachment.

As soon as the CNA left the room, I connected with St. Michael, the archangel, and asked him to tell me about the entity that had recently attached itself to my patient. I was told she was a twenty-four year old cocaine addict who had died in the E.D. several years earlier from an overdose. She worked as an independent high end prostitute to support her habit. I looked closer at this entity with the intent of seeing her true appearance—what she looked like when she was when alive. She was a very pretty woman with her olive complexion, brown hair, and brown eyes. I asked her telepathically who she was and why she was attaching to my patient. She remained silent, so I told her I could see her and that she could end up in a really bad place if she didn't cooperate with me.

She finally spoke up and in a very distressed tone of voice she said, "My name is Loretta, and I need a fix some kinda bad!"

I told her that I couldn't help her with that, but I could help her to move on to a beautiful place where she would never ever need or want another fix.

She replied, "No, no, no, you're trying to trick me! Lady, you don't understand; I've done some really bad things. I was a prostitute and did a lot drugs. The only place I would go to is hell, and I'm not going there. What business is it of yours if I hang around and live my life through this woman?"

I told her it was my business because "this woman" was my patient and she had no right to violate her free will and body. I continued to tell her that she would definitely go to heaven if she cooperated with me, but if she didn't St. Michael was standing by to take her to hell. I made sure she understood that either way, she had to go! Loretta started sobbing and begged me to please not send her to hell. I promised I wouldn't send her to hell, but she had to come out of Jenny's aura if she wanted to go to heaven. I also told her that God is gracious and loving and causes everyone to forget their mistakes in life so they can enjoy heaven—all she would have to do is accept the fact that she belongs in heaven.

She complied and as soon as she released herself completely back into the astral realm, I asked St. Michael to open up heaven so she could see where she was going. When heaven was laid open before her, she exclaimed, "Oh my, it's so beautiful!" Then she asked, "Am I really going to heaven?" I told her that St. Michael was by her side to lead her into heaven where she could stay for eternity or be reborn physically if she wanted to. I watched as she walked into heaven escorted by St. Michael and his angels. She was greeted by loved ones and ancestors who had passed away a long time ago. When the portal to heaven had closed, my patient woke up, looked at me with a smile on her face and said, "I'm so glad to see my favorite nurse. I'm glad you're taking care of me." I thought to myself, "Wow! What would she think if she knew that in addition to being her nurse, I was also her exorcist."

Gluttonous Ghosts Attached To George

George was a patient of mine on the medical-surgical unit of a small community hospital. He had been admitted to our unit with a diagnosis of morbid obesity and was scheduled to undergo gastric by-pass surgery, but he had five more pounds to lose before he could have the surgery.

On the first day I was assigned George as a patient, immediately upon walking into his room, I noticed three attachments in the area of his solar plexus chakra. The solar plexus chakra is located between the belly button and the breastbone. This chakra is associated with the lower back, the whole abdominal area, which includes the digestive system including liver, gallbladder, stomach and spleen as well as the kidneys and adrenal glands. Negative attachments in this chakra may lead to eating disorders—such as over eating and anorexia—digestive disorders, liver disease, gallbladder disease, spleen, and pancreatic problems such as diabetes. People with attachments to this area often suffer from low self-esteem and experience much anxiety. They also feel powerless to make positive changes in their lives.

The shape of each of these three attachments reminded me of the gluttonous green ghost from the popular 1984 movie, *Ghostbusters.* However, these ghostly attachments weren't green—they were solid black. I remember hesitating momentarily as I walked through George's door; I was completely startled by the appearance of three gigantic attached ghosts glaring out at me from his abdomen. I perceived that they feared they might be in trouble as soon as they saw me entering the room.

I ignored the attachments and went about introducing myself and completing my assessment. George was very sweet and talkative. He tried to smile often, but I could feel his emotional pain and sense of hopelessness regarding his situation. We talked about his weight loss goal and how much more he needed to lose to have the gastric bypass surgery. Instead of losing weight, he had actually gained five pounds in the last week and risked being discharged without any hope of surgery. I reminded him of what the doctor told him, that he might be in jeopardy of not having the surgery because he was gaining weight. When I asked him if he had someone sneaking food into the hospital, he broke down crying and said:

Ms. Shirl, I can't help myself. I feel like I'm going to die if I don't get something to eat when I feel the compulsion. I don't want to be like this. I was a football player in high school and I only weighed 175 pounds in my senior year. I can't believed I shot up to 720 pounds in three years. It doesn't even seem possible. I feel like I don't have any power over this hunger I have. It's like there's something inside of me that's taking control and making me eat all of the time. It's like I'm possessed. In my mind, I don't want to eat, but something compels me to do so anyway. I feel so hopeless to do anything about it.

I was amazed about his insight and how incredibly spot on he was about his condition. Up to this point, he had no way to validate his impression that something was possessing him and causing him to suffer. Now, I understood why the assignment was changed and I was given George as my patient when I had originally been assigned to work the outpatient chemotherapy unit that day. Divine intervention was at work and I had to do my part, not only as his nurse, but also as his deliverance minister. I knew I had to step up to the plate and that Spirit would protect me and my nursing job if I did.

I told George that in addition to being a nurse I had other abilities—that I was able to see he had three entities attached to him that were responsible for his eating compulsion. He stopped crying, looked up at me with a look of bewilderment and said, "What! Are you serious?" I told him I was very serious and his addiction to food had more to do with the energies attached to him than his own behavioral issues or compulsions. I told him I could get rid of them, but he would have to take measures to keep them away. He asked me how I knew he had these attachments and how I could get rid of them. I told him I had been able to see spirits for as long as I could remember and some people would call me a medium. He replied, "I don't care what you call it if you can help me." I asked him if he believed that I could get rid of them and he said, "Absolutely!"

I told him to hold my hand and close his eyes. I made contact with the three gluttonous ghosts and told them that they had to go immediately of their own volition or

I would have them removed and it would not go well for them. I also told them that if they were willing, I could cross them over into heaven where they would never be hungry again. They snorted and laughed at me saying, "We're not going anywhere and you can't make us. We like living through this man. He gives us everything we need. We're already in heaven." Then I knew they wouldn't co-operate with me, so I called on St. Michael, the Archangel and watched as he descended on a big white cloud with his army of warrior angels. Several of his angels took hold of the three evil entities, bound them with thick brown rope and cast them into a bottomless pit. Then they sealed it closed so that the gluttonous entities would never be able to return to the earth realm. I thanked God and St. Michael and asked them both to continue to protect George.

I asked George if he felt differently. He said, "I know this may sound ridiculous, but I feel like I just lost a hundred pounds. I don't feel the heaviness that I felt before." I told him that it didn't sound ridiculous at all because many people say they feel lighter after they've been delivered from spirit attachments. I told him it was important for him to guard his thoughts regarding food and to make healthy food choices. I also told him it was important for him to get both psychological and spiritual counseling so he could maintain a healthy mind and aura, both of which are vital in preventing attachments.

Within just a few days George lost seven pounds and was able to have his surgery two days later. I was his nurse on the day he returned from surgery. While I was doing his postoperative assessment, I noticed an entirely new spirit of gluttony floating in the astral realm above his head. It apparently was looking for a hole in which it could enter into his aura, but couldn't find one. I told the entity it could not have George and that I could help cross it over into heaven. It looked up at me and said, "Hell no! I'll just take you!" Then it tried to scare me by charging at me. I told the ghost it had just purchased a one way ticket to hell. Once again I called on St. Michael to come and remove the spirit and watched as he threw it into the pit. Then I knew George was going to be okay. His mind and aura had become healthy enough that it was difficult for the wandering spirit to find a way in.

I encountered George two years later at a spirit expo when he came to my table for a reading. He was happy, healthy, physically fit, and engaged to be married within a couple of weeks. He gave me a big hug and thanked me for allowing God to work through me to help him in his darkest hour.

You can Protect Yourself From Parasitic Hospital Ghosts

Hospital patients, visitors, and employees are constantly bombarded by exposure to all types of earthbound parasitic ghosts looking for someone to whom they can attach. There is no way to completely avoid being at a hospital, but there are methods of protection that can be implemented to help you avoid becoming a victim of nasty parasitic ghosts while at the hospital.

All living things are composed of energy that projects

an aura. The aura is a subtle energy field that surrounds the physical body and commonly extends anywhere from six inches to three feet from the body. Achieving and maintaining a healthy aura is the key to protection because it acts as a shield against parasitic ghosts. Since the aura is a reflection of the status of the mind, body and spirit of an individual, it is important to take care of all three aspects of your being. This is accomplished by feeding your mind with good thoughts, your body with healthy food, and your spirit with divine inspiration on a daily basis. However, when you're in a situation where your aura is compromised because of illness, extreme stress, or substances such as drugs and excessive alcohol, you can use several methods to instantly strengthen you aura. I refer to these protective methods as shielding-up. Several ways exist to shield-up, and one way is no better than the other. What is important is that the method resonates with you.

Methods to Shield Up

- **Bubble:** Visualize an iridescent bubble around yourself, protecting the outer edge of your aura with a strong and flexible membrane. Your bubble can be filled with any color that you choose, or it can be the colors of a rainbow. Make sure that your bubble goes all the way around, over your head, under your feet, behind and in front of you. State an affirmation that your bubble repels all negative energy, but allows positive energy to flow into it. After you create your bubble for the first time, all you have to do whenever you feel anxious, fearful or in the need for more protection, is see yourself inside your bubble and believe it is keeping negative energy out and allowing positive energy in.

- **Cloak or Shield:** Visualize a full-length, hooded cloak or a shield decorated with a protective design of your choice for protection, such as a cross or star of David. You can also use a 'mini shield' over any area that you feel is vulnerable, such as your solar plexus.

- **Crystals:** Crystals are amazing energy conduits. When charged with your prayerful intentions they can become a powerful amplifier of protective energy. Black tourmaline, black obsidian, blue kyanite, fluorite, labradorite, smoky quartz, hematite, apache tear, tiger's eye, and mica are wonderful stones for clearing negative energies. You can carry these crystals with you wherever you go.

- **Symbols**: Carry a symbol of protection such as a rune, a pentacle, a cross, or Star of David. A paper representation will do, but a piece of jewelry is nice. I like Kabbalah jewelry and find the amulets particularly effective for protection. Remember, it is important for your tools and techniques to resonate with you.

- **Angels:** Call on Archangel Michael for protection. You can ask Archangel Michael to use his sword to cut energetic chords, hooks, ties, and any negativity that may have attached to you during your hospitalization. I have found the following prayer to be very effective: *St. Michael the Archangel, defend us in battle, be our protection against the wickedness and snares of the devil. May God rebuke him we humbly pray; and do thou, O Prince of the Heavenly host, by the power of God, cast into hell Satan and all the evil spirits who prowl about the world seeking the ruin of souls. Amen.*

- **White Light:** Visualize a column of white light coming down from heaven and entering your body through the crown of your head. Watch as it spreads to the bottom of your feet and expands outside your body in all directions dissolving all negativity while strengthening your aura.

- **Shower:** Whenever you take a shower visualize the water flowing through your aura rinsing away any negative energy and taking it down the drain.

- **Essential Oils and Essences:** Put a drop of essential oil in the palm of your hand, then rub your hands together and pass them through your aura. Some good oils to use are lavender, frankincense, myrrh, sandalwood, eucalyptus, peppermint, bergamot, sage, and cedar.

Grounding & Centering

1. Sit or stand in a quiet place.
2. Take deep, slow breaths in through your nose and out through your mouth.
3. Visualize roots growing from the soles of your feet deep down into the center of the earth.
4. Watch as all negative energy leaves your body through these roots and is transmuted into positive healing energy in the molten core of the earth.
5. Now draw positive healing energy up from the earth and picture it as light coming up through the soles of your feet, pulsating through your legs, reaching your heart chakra and filling you with love for your own soul and body.
6. Watch as this light moves up to your crown chakra and shoots up in a column to the seventh spiritual plane where the Creator (God, Source) exists.
7. Bring the loving healing energy of the Creator down into the core of your body to heal you physically and strengthen your aura.
8. Bring your focus back to the present moment by becoming aware of your surroundings.

Spiritual energy has to be allowed to flow freely to work properly. That is why technique is very important when using this energy. For your shielding-up techniques to be effective, you need to understand how to tap into the power of God/Source/Universe through your subconscious mind. I would like to share with you the method I use to connect to the power of Source. It's based on the same visualization process used in all types of creative manifestation. You can use my method or any other method that resonates with you. These are the steps:

1. Sit, stand or lie in a relaxed position with your eyes closed.
2. Visualize the white light of creative power from the Creator/God/ Source entering your body through your nose (of course, if your nose is blocked, use your mouth) with every breath you take until it fills your whole body with light.
3. Then, visualize a column of white creative power coming down through the crown of your head, down into your neck, shoulders, chest, abdomen, pelvis, and hips until it fills the whole core of your body.
4. Next, visualize the white light of creative power as it flows down into your arms, and hands, then your feet and legs.
5. Finally, visualize the white light coursing out of the palms of your hands and soles of your feet, until it encases your body in a bubble of creative power that extends out at least three feet from you.
6. Open your eyes and clasp your hands together for a few seconds to seal the flow of creative energy

until you are ready to use it. You are now connected to the creative power of God. However, in order for the power to work, you must believe!

The Importance of Belief When Shielding-up

In spiritual work, you are dealing with the science of using the mind to manifest the outcome of your intentions. When thinking about your intentions, you are bound to sometimes face doubts and uncertainties. Do not be put off by these thoughts; instead use your mind to apply belief rather than giving up. Be positive and realize that these doubts and uncertainties are not true. Believe that the power within your subconscious mind can and will achieve whatever you wish, providing that you do not give way to doubt. The entire process of thinking deeply about your intention will send a signal to your subconscious mind that you are about to give it an instruction. Your subconscious mind cannot work with uncertainty, confusion, or constant changes of mind. An intention with firm and unwavering faith will clear a channel for the power within you to flow into manifestation!

About the Author

I am a natural psychic medium, which means that I was born able to perceive psychic information and communicate with the souls of people who have passed away. In addition to being a psychic medium, I am a wife, mother, grandmother, lecturer, author, registered nurse, and business woman. I hold a Bachelor of Science in Nursing, a Master's Degree in Business Administration, and another Master's Degree in the Science of Accounting. I live in the USA with my husband Joe and two cats, Zoey and Cecilia.

OTHER BOOKS BY SHIRLEY SMOLKO

A practicing Registered Nurse for close to three decades, Shirley Smolko—The Venetian Medium—is also a gifted Psychic Medium who has communicated with Spirit from the time she was five years old. In this captivating book, she shares her adventurous and incredible stories of contact with the Spirits. The fascinating story of her psychic

Cover Image by Shirley Smolko

odyssey offers illuminating insight into how we can better understand ourselves and our own psychic abilities. *Adventures of a Psychic Nurse: Spirits Everywhere!* may give you a new outlook on Life, Death, Spirits, Hauntings, Psychic Phenomena, and the Other Side!

Lightning Source UK Ltd.
Milton Keynes UK
UKHW020718311221
396440UK00012B/869